2

Reading for a Reason
Expanding Reading Skills

Laurie Blass
Elizabeth Whalley

Reading for a Reason Student Book 2: Expanding Reading Skills

ISBN: 0-07-294214-2
1 2 3 4 5 6 7 8 9 CCW/PCR 11 10 09 08 07 06 05

Editoral director: Tina Carver
Executive editor: Erik Gundersen
Development editor: Linda O'Roke
Photo researchers: David Averbach, David MacFarlane, Tobi Zausner
Production manager: MaryRose Malley
Interior designer: Monotype Composition
Cover designer: Monotype Composition

The **McGraw·Hill** Companies

Acknowledgements

The publisher and authors would like to thank the following education professionals whose comments, reviews, and assistance were instrumental in the development of *Reading for a Reason 2: Expanding Your Reading Skills.*

- ▶ Fairlie Atkinson, Sungkyunkwan University, Seoul, Korea

- ▶ Lynne Barsky, Suffolk County Community College, Jericho, NY

- ▶ Gerry Boyd, Northern Virginia Community College, Annandale, VA

- ▶ Donna Fujimoto, Osaka Jogakuin Daigaku, Osaka, Japan

- ▶ Ann-Marie Hadzima, National Taiwan University, Taipei, Taiwan, R.O.C.

- ▶ Patricia Heiser, University of Washington, Seattle, WA

- ▶ Yu-shen Hsu, Soochow University, Taipei, Taiwan, R.O.C.

- ▶ Greg Keech, City College of San Francisco, San Francisco, CA

- ▶ Irene Maksymjuk, Boston University, Boston, MA

- ▶ Yoshiko Matsubayashi, Kokusai Junior College, Tokyo, Japan

- ▶ Lorraine Smith, Adelphi University, Garden City, NY

- ▶ Leslie Eloise Somers, Miami-Dade County Public Schools, Miami, FL

- ▶ Karen Stanley, Central Piedmont Community College, Charlotte, NC

This book is dedicated to Improv Idols, the teachers at Bay Area Theater Sports.

Heartfelt thanks to the McGraw-Hill team, especially Erik Gundersen and Linda O'Roke, who helped shape this series and enhanced our enjoyment of the process.

The authors would like to thank all at the Plant, with special thanks to Frank and Gray for help with Chapter 5. We'd also like to thank Rachelle Waksler and the public libraries of Palo Alto and Menlo Park, California.

Table of Contents

Welcome to Reading for a Reason

Reading for a Reason 2: Expanding Reading Skills is the second in a three-level reading series that leads students to develop the critical reading and vocabulary skills they need to become confident, academic readers.

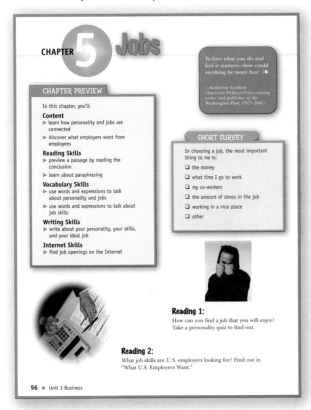

Chapter Preview boxes outline the main goals of the chapter and focus students' attention on what they will learn.

Short Surveys related to the chapter topic help students personalize the chapter content and activate prior knowledge.

Teaser photographs and questions pique students' interest.

Before You Read activities stimulate background knowledge, focus on vocabulary presentation and practice, and introduce important expressions.

Preview questions activate schemata and help students focus on the main idea of the passage.

Vocabulary Exercises preview the important words and expressions found in the readings.

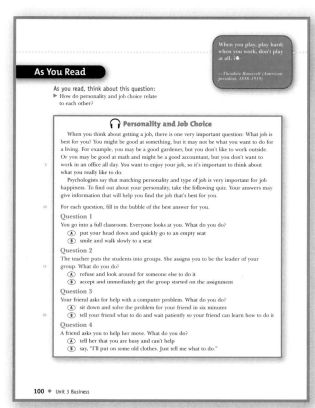

As You Read activities present readings that recycle reading skills and vocabulary to build reading fluency, and confidence, while increasing mastery.

Focus questions help students focus while reading, reinforce previewing skills, and build schemata.

First reading passage introduces the chapter topic in a short informal reading. Types of texts include emails, interviews, quizzes, and magazine articles.

After You Read activities focus on the main idea and details presented in Reading 1.

Standarized testing formats help students become familiar with a variety of test formats.

Talk About It activities facilitate group discussions on questions that help students synthesize, personalize, and extend concepts in the reading.

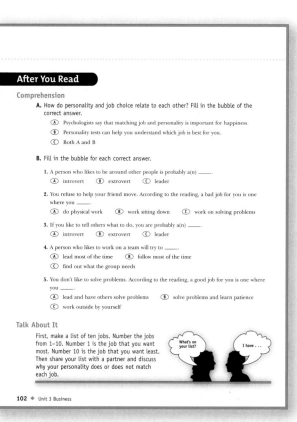

As You Read

As you read, think about this question:
► What do U.S. employers want from their employees?

> An individual's self-concept is the core of ... personality. It affects every aspect of human behavior: the ability to learn, the capacity to grow and change . . . A strong, positive self-image is the best possible preparation for success in life. ❧
>
> —*Joyce Brothers (American psychologist and author, b. 1928)*

What U.S. Employers Want

To get a great job, you need to show employers that you have what they are looking for. In the early 1990s, the United States Secretary of Commerce created a commission to look at what employers want from employees. This, along with other research, shows that all employers want the same things from employees. They want basic skills, thinking skills, and person-
5 al qualities, such as honesty and self esteem. Employers want these skills and qualities in all employees regardless of profession—from accountants to baseball players, computer workers to sales people, and chefs to teachers. Think about your strengths in these three areas when you look for a job. Be ready to talk about your strengths during a job interview. You want to be specific, so let's look closely at what employers want.

Basic Skills

10 Employers want people who know the basic skills of reading, writing, and arithmetic. They also want employees who listen and speak well.

To employers, reading means understanding written information. This information may be in sentences, paragraphs, charts, graphs, or schedules. Employees must be able to write messages, letters, directions, and reports. Sometimes, they must also be prepared to make
15 graphs and charts. For arithmetic, employers are looking for people who can add, subtract, multiply, and divide. Employees must know how to do percentages. They must be able to give estimates without a calculator.

Employers also want employees who can listen and respond to what someone says. In speaking, employers are looking for people who give information in an organized way. They
20 want employees to participate in discussions, and they especially like people who ask questions and can understand and use body language. Researchers say that 80 percent of the information in any face-to-face communication comes from body language, such as eye contact, posture, and facial expression. Employees must use body language to show speakers that
25 they are listening and that they understand the speaker.

Thinking Skills

There are six types of thinking skills that are important to employers: creative thinking, decision-making, problem-solving, seeing things in your mind's eye, knowing how to learn, and reasoning.

106 ◆ Unit 3 Business

Second reading passage introduces a longer academic, scientific, or formal reading on the chapter topic.

Focus questions help students focus while reading, and enforce and reinforce prediction skills.

Creative thinking means coming up with new ideas. Decision-making means thinking
30 about risks, evaluating alternatives, and choosing the best alternative. The first step in problem solving is recognizing that there is a problem. Then an employee has to find the reasons for the problem and think of a plan to solve it. In problem solving, the employee must also be willing to revise the solution if necessary. Employees who can see things in their mind's eye are able to picture a diagram and imagine the real object that it represents. They can also
35 imagine going through several steps in completing a job, even when reading about it or listening to someone explain it. Knowing how to learn means knowing how to find and learn new information. Reasoning means seeing the relationship between things; it means using logic to form conclusions. In addition, it means using old knowledge in new situations.

Personal Qualities

There are five personal qualities employers are looking for: responsibility, self-esteem,
40 sociability, self-management, and honesty.

To employers, responsibility means that an employee works hard to do an excellent job. The employee pays attention to details. The employee also does unpleasant tasks well. Of course, the employee comes on time and lets the employer know if there is a problem. Employers want people with self-esteem, people who like themselves. They want employees
45 with a positive self-image. Employees who are insecure make others uncomfortable. Friendliness and politeness are two aspects of sociability. Everyone likes to be around friendly and polite people. Employers don't want to tell employees what to do all the time, so they are looking for people with self-management skills. These people can set their own goals and meet those goals. People with good self-management skills don't show anger when someone
50 criticizes them. Honesty is also important. Everyone likes to be around people they trust.

Basic skills, thinking skills, and personality skills are the abilities needed in the 21st century workplace. Think of examples that you can use during a job interview to show that you have these skills.

Word Count: 686

Timed Reading

Read "What U.S. Employers Want" again. Read at a comfortable speed. Time your reading.

Start time: _____

End time: _____

My reading time: _____

Chapter 5 Jobs ◆ **107**

Headings, photographs, figures, and charts in the readings help students practice academic reading skills previously taught.

Timed Readings help students become aware of and improve their reading speed. Students chart their reading times in the Timed Reading Chart in the back of the book.

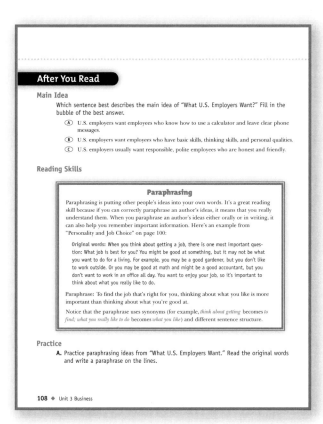

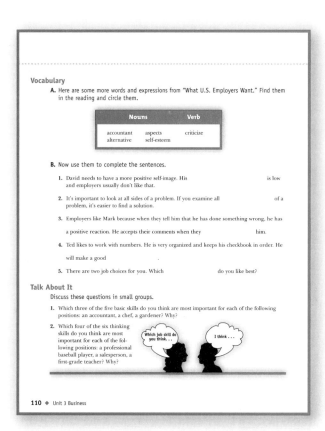

After You Read activities include extended vocabulary practice, reading skills presentation and practice, and collocation practice.

Main Idea questions allow students to check predictions made before the reading.

Reading Skills boxes present reading comprehension skills needed to succeed in an academic environment.

Vocabulary activities provide students with an opportunity to use words and phrases found in Reading 2.

Talk About It activities encourage discussions on questions that help students synthesize, personalize, and extend concepts in the reading.

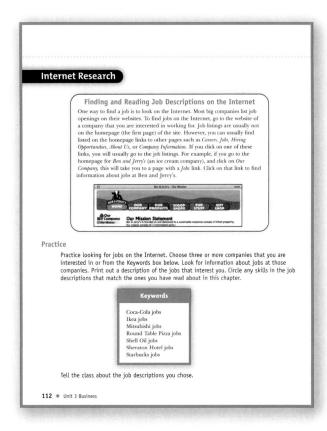

Finding and Reading Job Descriptions on the Internet

One way to find a job is to look on the Internet. Most big companies list job openings on their websites. To find jobs on the Internet, go to the website of a company that you are interested in working for. Job listings are usually not on the homepage (the first page) of the site. However, you can usually find listed on the homepage links to other pages such as *Careers, Jobs, Hiring Opportunities, About Us,* or *Company Information.* If you click on one of these links, you will usually go to the job listings. For example, if you go to the homepage for *Ben and Jerry's* (an ice cream company), and click on *Our Company,* this will take you to a page with a *Jobs* link. Click on that link to find information about jobs at Ben and Jerry's.

Practice

Practice looking for jobs on the Internet. Choose three or more companies that you are interested in or from the Keywords box below. Look for information about jobs at those companies. Print out a description of the jobs that interest you. Circle any skills in the job descriptions that match the ones you have read about in this chapter.

Keywords
Coca-Cola jobs
Ikea jobs
Mitsubishi jobs
Round Table Pizza jobs
Shell Oil jobs
Sheraton Hotel jobs
Starbucks jobs

Tell the class about the job descriptions you chose.

112 ◆ Unit 3 Business

Internet Research boxes present helpful tips on how to conduct academic research on the Internet.

Write About It activities allow students to write on different but related aspects of the chapter topic.

Writing A consists of two highly structured paragraph templates to provide guided writing experience.

Additional activities move students from models to less structured writings to open-ended writing activities.

Write About It

A. Write the following paragraphs. Fill in the blanks. Write complete sentences.

Paragraph One

I have skills and personal qualities that employers want. One of my basic skills is

_____
(List one basic skill)

For example, _____

_____
(Give an example of this skill)

My thinking skills include _____.
(List one thinking skill)

For example, _____

_____
(Give an example of this skill)

I have good personal qualities, too. One of my personal qualities is _____

_____
(Give an example of a personal quality)

For example, _____

_____
(Give an example of this quality)

Paragraph Two

My ideal job is _____
(Name your ideal job)

There are several reasons why this is my ideal job. One reason is (that) _____

_____
(Give one reason this is your ideal job)

Chapter 5 Jobs ◆ 113

On Your Own

Project

Design a job interview questionnaire and practice asking and answering the questions.

Step 1: Practice

Get into small groups. Think of a job and write a brief description of it. You may want to look at the results of the Internet search you did earlier. Next, write seven job interview questions for people who might want the job.

Examples:
1. Do you have good basic skills? Explain.
2. Give an example of your decision-making skills.
3. Are you an honest person? Give an example.

Step 2: Do the Interview

Meet with another group and get into pairs. Ask and answer the interview questions that your group wrote.

Step 3: Follow-Up

Evaluate your success. Which of your questions were good? Why? Which of your questions were not good? Why?

John Harrison
Edy's Ice Cream Tester

On Your Own is a structured speaking activity that helps students further explore each chapter theme.

Step 1 has students design a survey or prepare a presentation on the chapter topic.

Step 2 asks students to interview classmates using the questions they wrote in Step 1 or give their presentation to the class.

Step 3 allows students to explain the results of their survey or evaluate their presentations.

Wrap Up is an informal assessment tool that reviews chapter content, vocabulary, and reading skills.

Second Timed Reading focuses students' attention on their reading fluency by having them reread Reading 1 and Reading 2 and keep track of their times on the Timed Reading Chart in the back of the book.

Wrap Up

How Much Do You Remember?

Check your new knowledge. In this chapter you learned facts, words, and expressions. You also learned reading skills and you practiced writing. Complete the following to check what you remember.

1. If you are an *introvert*, what kind of job is good for you? _____

2. If you are an *extrovert*, what kind of job is good for you? _____

3. What are two parts of a reading passage that you can use to preview the passage? _____

4. What are *basic skills*? _____

5. What is *self-esteem*? _____

6. Use *decision-making* in a sentence. _____

7. How can you find job opportunities on the Internet? _____

Second Timed Readings

Now reread "Personality and Job Choice" and "What U.S. Employers Want." Time each reading separately. Write your times in the Timed Reading Chart on page 236.

Scope and Sequence

Vocabulary Skills	Writing Skills	Research Skills
▶ Using words and expressions to talk about college reading and reading techniques ▶ Using expressions to describe learning styles and techniques	▶ Explaining why a textbook is easy or difficult to read ▶ Writing about a favorite type of reading material	▶ Learning to read a webpage ▶ Interviewing people about their favorite type of reading
▶ Using words and expressions to talk about types of tests and test-taking strategies ▶ Using two-word verbs to discuss tests and test-taking	▶ Explaining how to prepare for a test ▶ Comparing types of tests	▶ Evaluating URLs in search results ▶ Interviewing people about their favorite type of test
▶ Using words and expressions to talk about trade and travel in the past ▶ Using expressions with *travel* to talk about traveling over time and places	▶ Writing about cross-cultural exchange in the past ▶ Writing about your favorite time in history	▶ Find biographies on the Internet ▶ Asking people about their favorite person in history
▶ Using words and expressions to talk about airplanes and flying ▶ Using expressions for movement	▶ Describing a memory of flying ▶ Describing an image that depicts a moment in aviation history	▶ Finding images on the Internet ▶ Researching and presenting your ideas on improving air travel
▶ Using words and expressions to talk about personality and jobs ▶ Using words and expressions to talk about job skills	▶ Describing your skills and personal qualities ▶ Writing about your ideal job	▶ Finding and reading job descriptions on the Internet ▶ Asking and answering job interview questions
▶ Using words and expressions to talk about marketing and culture ▶ Using verb + infinitive combinations to discuss international marketing	▶ Explaining what international marketers do in order to sell products overseas ▶ Describing a successful company, product, product name, or ad	▶ Limiting search results ▶ Designing and presenting an ad

Scope and Sequence

Vocabulary Skills	Writing Skills	Internet and Research Skills
▶ Using words and expressions to discuss the influence of Mars on everyday life, space exploration, and the geography of Mars ▶ Using expressions to make comparisons	▶ Describing a favorite book, movie, or TV program about space, space exploration, aliens, or Mars ▶ Expressing and supporting your opinion of space exploration	▶ Focusing an Internet search ▶ Conducting a survey on the value of space exploration
▶ Using words and expressions to describe weather and weather predictions ▶ Using verb phrases to talk about the weather and weather emergencies	▶ Describing the weather in two places on the same date ▶ Describing your favorite type of weather and explaining why you like it	▶ Using the Internet to find climate and weather information ▶ Collecting and presenting information on the weather in 7 international cities
▶ Using words and expressions to talk about the life of a jazz musician and the development of jazz ▶ Using prepositions with time expressions	▶ Describing a favorite type of music ▶ Discussing the types of music that contributed to jazz	▶ Using an online music dictionary ▶ Preparing a presentation on a favorite piece of music
▶ Using words and expressions to talk about art and artists ▶ Using expressions to discuss artistic influences	▶ Writing about a favorite work of art and explaining why it's your favorite ▶ Analyzing characteristics of *Japonisme* in a work of art	▶ Finding a specific word or phrase on a webpage ▶ Researching and giving a presentation on an artist or a work of art

To the Teacher

Series Overview

Reading for a Reason: Expanding Reading Skills is a three-level academic theme-based reading series that focuses on cross-curricular content and promotes critical thinking skills. The series is designed to enhance the academic reading and vocabulary skills of English language learners. The three books in the series range from High-Beginning to High-Intermediate.

- ▶ Reading for a Reason 1—High-Beginning
  Reading passage word count 150–600

- ▶ Reading for a Reason 2—Intermediate
  Reading passage word count 425–950

- ▶ Reading for a Reason 3—High-Intermediate
  Reading passage word count 550–1500

The objectives of *Reading for a Reason* are to increase students' independence, confidence, competence, and comfort in reading in English and in learning new vocabulary. To be successful academically, students must have strong reading, vocabulary, and computer skills. *Reading for a Reason* is designed to work on the skills that are most needed for academic success.

To be independent readers, students need to be able to self-activate schemata and use critical thinking skills. Therefore, each book in the series promotes critical thinking skills before, during, and after the readings. The critical thinking skills include annotating a text, analyzing graphics, and identifying fact and opinion. The readings encompass a wide range of academic disciplines: biology, cultural anthropology, history, psychology, science, business, and sociology. Chapters recycle reading skills (such as using titles, headings, and captions to predict) taught in previous chapters. Thus, students not only have opportunities to practice skills when they are taught, but they are given additional practice in later chapters using new academic content. Students are also able to self-monitor their reading speed by filling in the chart of timed readings. Intrinsically interesting content keeps students' attention as they develop their vocabulary and reading power.

Organization of the Book

Reading for a Reason 2 is an intermediate level book that prepares students for the academic reading they will have to do once they have begun their academic coursework. *Reading for a Reason 2* features five units that span a variety of academic disciplines. Each unit begins with an introduction to the academic discipline including a definition and explanation, a list of important people in the field, and key questions students answer to discover if they are attracted to the discipline. The unit also includes two twenty-page chapters that integrate reading content with reading, vocabulary, speaking, writing, and Internet research skills.

Each chapter has the following components:

- **What do you think?** promotes interactive pair work that personalizes the chapter topic in more depth.

- **Before You Read** stimulates background knowledge, focuses on vocabulary presentation and practice, and introduces important expressions.

- **Reading 1** introduces the chapter topic in a short informal reading. Types of texts include emails, interviews, quizzes, and magazine articles.

- **Reading 2** introduces a longer, academic, scientific, or formal reading on the chapter topic.

- **Timed Reading** helps students become aware of and improve their reading speed by timing themselves and charting their times on the Timed Reading Chart in the back of the book.

- **Reading Skills** box presents reading comprehension skills needed to succeed in an academic environment.

- **After You Read** includes extended vocabulary practice, reading skills presentation and practice, as well as practice with collocations.

- **Talk About It** permits group discussions on questions that help students synthesize, personalize, and extend concepts in the reading.

- **Expressions** present collocations from Reading 1 and Reading 2. Practice exercises follow each box.

- **Internet Research** presents helpful tips on how to conduct academic research on the Internet. Practice exercises follow each box.

- **Write About It** allows students to write at least three different paragraphs on aspects related to the chapter topic.

- **On Your Own** presents structured speaking activities that help students further explore each chapter theme.

- **Wrap Up** is an informal assessment tool that reviews chapter content, collocations, and reading skills.

- **Crossword Puzzle** reviews vocabulary taught in the chapter.

Audio Program

Each *Reading for a Reason* student book is paired with an audio program available on both audio CD and audiocassette. The audio program allows students to listen to the 20 reading passages as they read. Research shows that different students learn in different ways. By allowing students both visual and aural input, the audio program strengthens the skill set of both auditory and visual learners. Recorded readings will also enhance aural/oral skills (reception and production) with regard to the vocabulary presented in the series. This also facilitates pronunciation of individual words as well as stress, intonation, and other suprasegmentals associated with collocations. Studies have also shown that listening to readings can help increase reading speed because English language learners unconsciously speed up when listening to a normal-paced recording of text.

Teacher's Manuals

Each book in the series also has a Teacher's Manual that contains a complete answer key to the student book and chapter quizzes. The chapter quizzes consist of an additional reading passage on the chapter topic, five comprehension questions that reinforce the reading skills taught within the chapter, and five vocabulary questions. Quizzes can be photocopied and given to students for either review or assessment.

Think About Your Reading Skills

Think about your reading skills. Read the following statement and check the words that best describe you.

Before I begin a reading passage, I . . .	Never	Sometimes	Always
think about my personal connection to the passage topic.	_____	_____	_____
ask myself questions about the title of the passage.	_____	_____	_____
read the headings and subheadings in the passage.	_____	_____	_____
look at photos, charts, or tables and read their captions.	_____	_____	_____
read and think about the passage introduction.	_____	_____	_____
read the topic sentences of all the paragraphs.	_____	_____	_____

As I read a passage, I . . .	Never	Sometimes	Always
identify the main idea.	_____	_____	_____
identify details.	_____	_____	_____
identify examples.	_____	_____	_____
identify facts and opinions.	_____	_____	_____
take notes in the margin.	_____	_____	_____
guess the meanings of new words by using the context (the surrounding words) of each one.	_____	_____	_____

After I read a passage, I . . .	Never	Sometimes	Always
make a summary of what I read.	_____	_____	_____
predict questions about it that might be on a test.	_____	_____	_____
read it again.	_____	_____	_____

Skilled readers try to use the reading skills above as much as possible. If you don't, try to practice the skills listed *before, as,* and *after* you read.

1 Student Success

What is Student Success?

Student success describes when students do well in school. Students who do well in school usually also have job success, positive attitudes, and good relationships with others. Successful students know how to:

- read and take notes
- manage their time
- use the library efficiently
- write clearly
- study effectively
- do well on tests
- ask questions in class

People have been interested in successful learning since ancient times. As the Chinese philosopher Confucius (551–479 B.C.) said, "Learning without thought is labor lost."

SOME FAMOUS PEOPLE WHO DID WELL IN SCHOOL

William Wordsworth—English poet, 1770–1850

Marie Curie—Polish physicist, 1867–1934

Maria Tallchief—Native American ballerina, 1925–

Kofi Annan—Ghanaian, Secretary General of the United Nations, 1938–

Antonia Novello—Puerto Rican American, former Surgeon General of the United States, 1944–

William Jefferson Clinton—American, former president of the United States, 1946–

Benazir Bhutto—Pakistani, former Prime Minister of Pakistan, 1953–

Student Success and You

If you are successful in school, you can go into any field that interests you, such as accounting, computer science, engineering, journalism, business, medicine, space exploration, or teaching.

In this unit you will be introduced to strategies successful students use. Ask yourself these questions:

- Do I want to become a better reader?
- Do I want to succeed on tests?
- Do I enjoy asking questions?
- Do I want to get good grades?
- Do I want to learn to manage my time better?

How to Read a Textbook

CHAPTER PREVIEW

In this chapter, you'll:

Content
▶ read emails between students who discuss all the reading they have to do

▶ discover how to become an active reader and learn a five-part reading system

Reading Skills
▶ prepare yourself physically and mentally for reading

▶ identify the main idea of a reading

Vocabulary Skills
▶ use words and expressions to talk about college-level reading and reading techniques

▶ use expressions to describe learning styles and techniques

Writing Skills
▶ write about your favorite kind of reading material and what makes something easy or difficult to read

Internet Skills
▶ scan a webpage to find important information

> A book is like a garden carried in a pocket. ❧
>
> —*Chinese proverb*

SHORT SURVEY

My favorite thing to read is a(n):

❑ email

❑ website

❑ newspaper

❑ magazine

❑ textbook

❑ novel

❑ other _____

Reading 1:
What do two students think about all the reading they have to do for college? Read their emails to find out.

Reading 2:
Is it possible to make reading textbooks easier? "Active Reading" has the answer.

What do you think?

Read the statements and circle the words that describe your textbook reading style. Then ask your partner about his or her reading style. Discuss your answers.

When I begin reading a textbook passage, I . . .

I . . .

My Textbook Reading Style

Before I begin reading a textbook passage, I:

see how many pages there are.
Never   Sometimes   Always

find a comfortable place to sit.
Never   Sometimes   Always

look quickly at every page.
Never   Sometimes   Always

ask myself, "Why am I reading this?"
Never   Sometimes   Always

As I read a textbook passage, I:

think about the ideas in the reading and connect them to other things that I know about.
Never   Sometimes   Always

see pictures of the ideas in my head.
Never   Sometimes   Always

look for keywords.
Never   Sometimes   Always

make an outline of the main ideas from the reading.
Never   Sometimes   Always

After I read a textbook passage, I:

repeat out loud and in my own words the main ideas.
Never   Sometimes   Always

read it again.
Never   Sometimes   Always

Reading 1: I Can't Believe How Much Reading We Have to Do!

Before You Read

Preview

A. The title of Reading 1 is "I Can't Believe How Much Reading We Have to Do!" It is an exchange of emails between friends. What do you think the friends are talking about in their emails? Discuss your ideas with a partner.

B. What are the most difficult things about school for you? Read the items in this list. Circle the answers that are true for you.

3 = very difficult	2 = somewhat difficult	1 = not difficult	0 = doesn't apply to me
1. Reading textbooks	3 2	1	0
2. Writing papers	3 2	1	0
3. Speaking in class	3 2	1	0
4. Studying for tests	3 2	1	0
5. Memorizing information	3 2	1	0
6. Taking tests	3 2	1	0
7. Doing research	3 2	1	0
8. Being away from home and family	3 2	1	0
9. Distractions (new friends, parties)	3 2	1	0
10. Other _____	3 2	1	0

C. What strategies (techniques) do you use to help make these things easier? Share your strategies with your partner.

Vocabulary

Here are some words and expressions from "I Can't Believe How Much Reading We Have to Do!" Read the sentences. Match each underlined word or expression with the correct definition in the box.

> a. criticize yourself   c. in the same situation   e. say out loud
> b. finish it   d. look at   f. works

___C___ 1. I'm <u>in the same boat</u> as you: I have a lot of homework this weekend, too.

_____ 2. Don't <u>be hard on yourself</u>. You're a good student!

_____ 3. This study technique <u>is tried and true</u>—I've seen it succeed many times.

_____ 4. I have too much work! I don't know how I'll <u>get it done</u>.

_____ 5. Tell me what the chapter is about. <u>Recite</u> the main ideas to me.

_____ 6. I'm not going to read the chapter right now. I'm just going to <u>survey</u> the pictures and the headings.

As you read, think about this question:

▶ What is Ashley's technique for reading textbooks?

🎧 I Can't Believe How Much Reading We Have to Do!

Ashley and Tony are old friends. They go to the same college and take some of the same classes. They email each other almost every day. In their emails, they talk about school. They describe the things they like and complain about the things they don't like. They share ideas and help each other.
Here are some of their emails:

#1

5   From: Tony Hernandez <hernandez@rccc.edu>
Date: Monday, January 30, 2008 9:05 PM
To: Ashley Chen <achen@rccc.edu>
Subject: I Can't Believe How Much Reading We Have to Do!

Hi Ashley,

10   What do you think of your classes this semester? I like most of mine, but it's so early in the semester, and we have so much work to do. I can't believe how much reading we have to do!

I have to read 150 pages this week! I have to do that and do all my other work too—a lab report and an essay!

15   You're such a good student. And you were always a good reader. You know I'm not much of a reader... I never even read books for fun! What am I going to do? How am I going to get all this reading done?

Tony

From: Ashley Chen <achen@rccc.edu>
Date: Monday, January 30, 2008 10:05 PM
To: Tony Hernandez <hernandez@rccc.edu>
Subject: Re: I Can't Believe How Much Reading We Have to Do!

Hi Tony,

I told you it was going to get hard, didn't I? I'm in the same boat—I've got over 100 pages to read by Thursday.

Yes, you know how much I used to love reading! I used to read novels all the time. Now I never read them—I only have time to read textbooks. It's much harder to read a textbook than a novel.

But don't be so hard on yourself. You're smart, Tony! There are some techniques for reading textbooks. You just have to learn them. One thing I know for sure—you have to have a positive attitude about reading. Also, don't read when you're tired.

Ashley

#2

From: Tony Hernandez <hernandez@rccc.edu>
Date: Monday, January 30, 2008 11:35 PM
To: Ashley Chen <achen@rccc.edu>
Subject: Re: I Can't Believe How Much Reading We Have to Do!

O.K., I get it. But I need some more of your secret techniques. What are they? I need to learn them fast!

Tony

#3

From: Ashley Chen <achen@rccc.edu>
Date: Monday, January 30, 2008 11:55 PM
To: Tony Hernandez <hernandez@rccc.edu>
Subject: Re: I Can't Believe How Much Reading We Have to Do!

#4

45   They're not secrets. In fact, I use the one we learned in high school. (I guess you were absent that day!) It's tried and true—my father said he used it in college, too. You just have to do it. It's called the "SQ3R" reading system. *S* is for "survey." It means, when you have a textbook chapter to read, first you look at all the headings, pictures, charts, captions, and stuff like that. *Q* is for
50   "questions." Find the main ideas and ask yourself questions about them. The three *Rs* are "read"—read the stuff; "recite"—say the main ideas in your own words; and "review"—review what you just read.

Try it! There are other techniques, too. I'll tell you about them when we get together to study on Wednesday.

55   Ashley

Word Count: 626 words

Timed Reading

Read "I Can't Believe How Much Reading We Have to Do!" again. Read at a comfortable speed. Time your reading.

Start time: _____ *(11:08)*

End time: _____ *(11:13)*

My reading time: _____ *(5 minutes)*

Students usually have to read a lot. In each chapter, you will be asked to do four timed readings. These timed readings will help you increase your reading speed.

After You Read

Comprehension

A. Fill in the bubble of the sentence that best describes the main idea of the emails between Ashley and Tony.

- (A) There's a lot of reading in college, and if you're not a good reader, you're going to have a hard time.
- (B) There's a lot of reading in college, but there are techniques for making it easier.
- (C) There's a lot of reading in college, but you don't have to do all of it.

B. Fill in the bubble for each correct answer.

1. Tony is worried because _____.

- (A) he has to do a lab report and an essay this week
- (B) he has to read 150 pages and do a lab report and an essay this week
- (C) he has to read 150 pages in a textbook this week

2. From her email, you can guess that Ashley has _____.

- (A) a situation that is similar to Tony's
- (B) more work than Tony
- (C) less work than Tony

3. Which statement is probably true?

- (A) In the past, Ashley read a lot for fun.
- (B) In the past, Tony read a lot for fun.
- (C) In the past, Ashley and Tony had to read more textbooks than they do now.

4. Which statement is probably NOT true?

- (A) Tony thinks Ashley is a good reader.
- (B) Tony feels bad about his reading ability.
- (C) Ashley thinks Tony isn't very smart.

Talk About It

Discuss the following questions with a partner.

1. Do you think textbooks are difficult to read? If yes, why? If not, why not?

2. Have you used the SQ3R technique? Does it work for you?

Reading 2: Active Reading

Before You Read

Preview

A. The title of Reading 2 is "Active Reading." What do you think "active reading" means? Try to think of an example. Discuss your ideas with a partner.

> Reading is to the mind what exercise is to the body. 🐚
>
> —*Joseph Addison (British politician and writer, 1672–1719)*

B. Preview these words or expressions from the reading. Complete each sentence below with the correct word or expression.

analyze	comprehend	concepts	~~demanding~~
enormous	link	paraphrase	take a break

1. Tony didn't know that college homework would be so difficult. He didn't think it would be

   _____*demanding*_____ at all, so he was very surprised.

2. Tony decided to use the word "_____" instead of "ideas" in his history paper because it sounded better.

3. Ashley has to read 400 pages this week. That's an _____ amount!

4. Ashley wanted to stop reading for a while, so she decided to _____

   _____ _____ when she was halfway through the chapter.

5. Diagrams often help you understand the information in a chapter. In fact, textbook authors

   usually use them to help the reader _____ difficult ideas.

6. The professor wanted Tony to explain the ideas in his own words, so she asked him to

   _____ the main ideas of the chapter that was assigned as homework.

7. Try to _____ your own experience to the information in a reading passage. Connecting what you already know to the ideas in a passage makes it easier to understand.

8. Ashley needed to examine carefully a difficult problem from class, so she read the textbook to

   help her _____ it.

Reading Skills

Getting Ready to Read

Good readers prepare themselves for reading both physically and psychologically.

Physical Preparation: To prepare physically to read, make sure that you are sitting in a comfortable chair. If you are reading a textbook and need to take notes, try sitting at a desk. Make sure you have good light. The light should be behind you and to the side so that it shines on the book. Your head should not make a shadow on the page. Read in a quiet place unless you can "tune out" (ignore) noise and like to read in a café or coffee shop. Take a break from your reading about every 45 minutes.

Psychological Preparation: Psychological preparation is also important, especially if you have a lot of reading to do. First, think about why you are doing the reading. Ask yourself, "Why am I reading this? What do I want to know when I am finished?" Be positive. Feel that you will accomplish your reading goals and that you will know what you want to know when you are finished. If you are having trouble understanding your reading, take a break. Go back to the hard parts and reread them later.

Practice

This week keep a reading journal. Practice reading in four different settings, including the example that is given in the chart below. Record ideas about how you prepare to read and whether or not each setting is right for you.

Place and Time of Day	Type of Chair and/or Desk	Lighting	Noise Level	Purpose of Reading	How Did I Feel?/ What Did I Do?
Library 4–6 p.m.	Sat at library table Very comfortable	Good	Quiet most of the time	To get information for an essay	Nervous; difficult topic Took two breaks

As you read, think about this question:
► How can you be an active reader?

> When I am reading a book, whether wise or silly, it seems to be alive and talking to me. ❧
>
> —*Jonathan Swift (British author, 1667–1745)*

🎧 Active Reading

The amount of reading that college students must do is enormous and demanding. It's easy to get discouraged, but most experts agree that reading actively is the key to understanding what you read. Having a set of active reading strategies and a reading system are a couple of ways that good readers approach textbook reading.

Active Reading Strategies

5   Here are some strategies for reading actively and getting the most out of your reading.

► **Take Frequent Breaks**—When you have a lot to read, try to schedule a short stretching break about every 40 minutes. A person's brain retains information best in short study segments. Also, if you're having trouble with some difficult concepts, take a break and come back to them later.

10 ► **Make Connections with the Material**—Try to link new information with what you already know. To make associations and jog your memory, ask yourself the following questions:

- What conclusions can I make as I survey the material?
- How can I apply this new material to other material, concepts, and examples?
15 - What are some examples of the concepts in the reading? What are some examples that are the opposite of the concepts?
- What has been my past experience with readings on similar subjects?
- What do I already know about the topic? How might this influence my approach to the reading?

20 ► **Talk with the Author**—That's right—have an imaginary conversation with the author as you read. Form a picture of the author in your mind. What questions do you have for him or her? Which of his or her ideas do you agree with? Which do you disagree with? Write these down in the margins.

► **Keep Learning Styles in Mind as You Read**—People learn in different ways. Visual
25 learners like pictures. Auditory learners like to learn by hearing information. Kinesthetic learners learn by doing. If you're visual, form pictures in your head as you read. If you're auditory, read the material into a tape recorder and listen to it later. If you're kinesthetic, present and summarize your material for your study group. Regardless of your style, use all three methods to vary your reading experience and see the material in
30 a different way.

The Five-Part Reading System

In addition to being an active reader, it's a good idea to have a reading system. One of the methods that good readers use is the Five-Part Reading System (see Figure 1). It works well with active reading strategies.

Here's how it works:

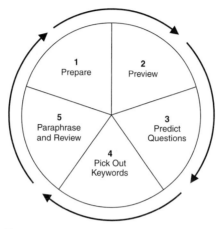

Figure 1

35 **Part 1: Prepare**—Try to prepare yourself mentally for reading by creating a positive and interested attitude. You will remember more if you have a positive attitude. Focus your attention on what you are going to read. Think about your purpose for reading and what you will do with the information. Are you reading to find facts? Get background information? Memorize formulas and data? Are you reading to analyze and comprehend a complex sub-
40 ject? Think about what you may already know about the subject before you begin reading. (See "Make Connections with the Material," page 14.) Also, prepare yourself physically. Read when you have plenty of energy and where you will not be distracted. Sit in a comfortable chair and take deep breaths when you want to reenergize yourself.

Part 2: Preview—Previewing is a major step in getting the most from your reading. Just as
45 an athlete warms up before running, previewing warms up your brain for incoming information. The goal in previewing is to read quickly to get an overall understanding of the main ideas. For example, if you have a chapter to read, pay attention to the title, the introduction, the chapter objectives, the main ideas, and keywords. Look for illustrations, pictures, figures, charts, and tables. Pay attention to boldface words: these are often the key-
50 words in the reading. All of these elements give you an idea about the main ideas of the material that you are going to read.

Part 3: Predict Questions—Asking questions about the material before you read and as you read has many benefits. It gets you interested, keeps you focused, helps you organize information, and helps you prepare for tests. Before you read, look at each section heading and turn it into a question. For example, if the section heading is "The Risks of Ignoring Culture," ask yourself: What are the risks of ignoring culture? As you read, predict test questions and search for the answers. Ask yourself: Who? What? Where? When? Why? and How? Jot down your questions in the margin of the book or in your reading notes. The more questions you ask, the better prepared you will be to find answers and the more prepared you will be for test questions.

Part 4: Pick out Keywords—Find keywords, main ideas, definitions, facts, main concepts, supporting points, and answers to the questions you asked. There are many ways to do this. You can write in the margins, take notes on index cards, draw pictures, and underline or highlight important material. Also, make an outline as you read. Outlining helps you simplify and organize information. In addition, the physical process of writing and organizing material helps you remember it.

Part 5: Paraphrase—Paraphrase, summarize, and review the reading material. Paraphrasing as you read makes you an active reader. As you read, it will help you to remember main points. At the ends of major sections, recite in your own words the main points of each section. After you read, write a short summary and then recite it aloud as well. Review your summary several times until you understand the material and can explain it to someone else. Organize study groups and take turns reviewing and listening to each other's summaries.

Word Count: 949

Source: *Peak Performance: Success in College and Beyond* (Ferret)

Timed Reading

Read "Active Reading" again. Read at a comfortable speed. Time your reading.

Start time: _____

End time: _____

My reading time: _____

After You Read

Identifying the Main Idea

When you read, it's important to get the main idea of a passage. The main idea is the writer's general message. Usually, there is a main idea to the whole reading. Major sections of a reading may each have a main idea. Individual paragraphs in the reading may also have a main idea. These ideas are called "supporting ideas" because they support the main idea of the whole reading.

Authors often state the main idea of a passage in the introduction—but not always. Main ideas of paragraphs and sections can be at the beginning, in the middle, or at the end. If you can't find the main idea, ask yourself, "What is the author's main point? Why did he or she write this?"

Practice

Find the sentence in "Active Reading" that states the main idea and underline it. Then answer these questions:

1. Where in the passage did you find it? _____

_____

2. Which statement below best describes the main idea of "Active Reading"? Fill in the bubble of the correct answer.

(A) College students have to do an enormous amount of reading.

(B) Good readers often use active reading strategies and a reading system when they read textbooks.

(C) College students are easily discouraged by the amount that they have to read.

Getting the Details

A. Fill in the bubble for each correct answer.

1. Which statement is true?
- Ⓐ You can remember information better if you study for longer time periods.
- Ⓑ You can remember information better if you study for shorter time periods.
- Ⓒ You can remember information better if you do not take breaks.

2. Which statement is NOT true?
- Ⓐ If you're having trouble with your reading, take a short stretching break.
- Ⓑ If you're having trouble with your reading, it's best to stay with it until you finish.
- Ⓒ If you're having trouble with your reading, do something else for a while and come back to it later.

3. Which is an example of "making a connection with the reading material"?
- Ⓐ thinking about a book you have read in the past on a similar topic
- Ⓑ reading the material into a tape recorder
- Ⓒ taking a break every 40 minutes

4. What does it mean to "form a picture in your mind of the author"?
- Ⓐ As you read, occasionally look at the author's photo on the back of the book.
- Ⓑ Draw a picture of what your think the author looks like while you are reading.
- Ⓒ Imagine the author as a person you can talk to.

5. Which statement is true?
- Ⓐ Visual learners learn by doing.
- Ⓑ Kinesthetic learners learn with pictures.
- Ⓒ Auditory learners learn by hearing information.

B. Fill in the following chart with at least two examples from each part of the Five-Part Reading System.

Parts	Examples
Part 1: Prepare	*have a positive attitude; sit in a comfortable chair*
Part 2: Preview	
Part 3: Predict Questions	
Part 4: Pick out Keywords	
Part 5: Paraphrase	

Vocabulary

A. Here are some expressions from "Active Reading." Find them in the reading and circle them.

come back to

getting the most out of

get discouraged about

jot down

warms up

B. Now use them to complete the sentences.

1. A good reader _____ _____ before reading, just as a runner does before a race.

2. As you read a textbook, it's a good idea to _____ _____ the main ideas on a piece of paper.

3. Don't _____ _____ _____ all the reading you have to do. Have a positive attitude and a reading system, and everything will be fine!

4. For _____ _____ _____ _____ _____ your reading, be an active reader.

5. After you have a rest, _____ _____ _____ your reading, and it will be easier to understand.

Expressions

Expressions about Learning Skills

Here are some expressions from Reading1 and Reading 2. They describe types of learners and learning techniques.

Types of Learners	Learning Techniques	
auditory learners	do something physical	jog your memory
kinesthetic learners	focus your attention	make associations
visual learners	form a picture in your mind	prepare (yourself) mentally
	have a positive attitude	

Example: Kinesthetic learners like to do something physical as they learn.

Practice

A. Find and underline each learning skills expression from the box above in "I Can't Believe How Much Reading We Have to Do" or "Active Reading."

B. Now use some of them to complete the sentences.

1. If you're a visual learner, you _____ _____ _____ _____

   _____ _____ of the information that you are reading about.

2. Try not to be negative about your reading. If you _____ _____

   _____ _____, you will remember more of what you read.

3. _____ _____ learn better when they can see the information.

4. To prepare, _____ _____ with the passage. For example, try to connect it to something else that you read on the same topic.

5. Athletes prepare themselves physically by warming up. Readers _____ themselves

   _____ by thinking about a passage before they read it.

6. When you read, try taking notes. The notes will help to _____ _____

   _____ when you review the material for a test.

Internet Research

How to Read a Webpage

Reading a website requires scanning skills. Scanning is moving your eyes quickly over a page to find specific information, such as a number or a name. It helps you find information on a website (often called just a *site*) and decide quickly if it is useful to you. To do this, you scan the homepage of a site for the following details:

► **Site Name:** Every site has a name. It appears in the top margin of your browser as the page is loading.

► **Page Name:** The page may also have a name that describes the information on that particular page, just like the title of an article or a document.

► **Navigation Links:** These tell you the main areas or sections of the site. Navigation links are usually on the left-hand side of the page, at the top, or across the bottom.

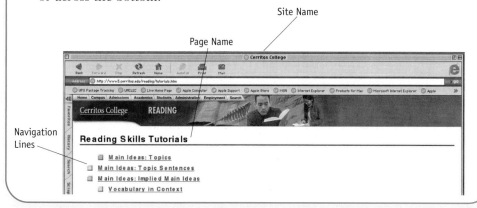

Practice

Practice scanning a webpage. Go to the homepage of a tried-and-true website such as cnn.com, your school website, or a government website such as nasa.gov. Scan the webpage to answer the questions below. Print a copy of the webpage and bring it to class.

1. Identify the site name, the page name (if there is one), and the navigation links. Did these help you decide if the page was useful?

2. In your opinion, is it easy to find information on this page? Why or why not?

Tell the class about the webpage.

Write About It

A. Write the following paragraphs. Fill in the blanks. Write complete sentences.

Paragraph One

My _____ textbook is very easy/difficult to read.
(Insert type of book, e.g. history)   (Circle one)

It's easy/difficult because _____.
(Circle one)   (Explain the reason)

For example, _____.
                    (Give an example from the book that supports this reason)

Also, it's _____.
                          (Explain another reason)

An example of this is (that) _____.
                    (Give an example from the book that supports this reason)

Paragraph Two

My favorite kind of reading material is _____.
                                    (Insert favorite type of reading material)

It's my favorite because _____.
                              (Give one reason that you like this type)

For example, _____.
                        (Give an example that supports this reason)

Another reason that I enjoy reading _____
                                      (Repeat favorite type of material)

is (that) _____.
                    (Give another reason that you like this type)

For example, _____.
                        (Give an example that supports this reason)

B. Now write your own paragraphs. Write one paragraph about what makes textbooks easy or difficult to read and another about your favorite type of reading material.

C. Write more paragraphs about reading and reading skills. Use five words and expressions from this chapter and your Internet research.

On Your Own

Project

Do an interview. Ask a classmate about his or her reading habits.

Step 1: Practice

Listen as your teacher reads the interview questions. Do you understand them? Repeat them with your teacher so you can pronounce them correctly.

Step 2: Do an Interview

Ask a classmate about his or her reading habits. Fill in the chart below.

Reading Interview

Name: _____

1. What is your favorite type of reading material?

   _____

2. Why is this your favorite thing to read?

   _____

3. What is the best example of this type of reading material?

   _____

4. In a week, how much reading to you do for school?

   _____

5. What strategies do you use when you have to read for school?

   _____

   _____

Step 3: Follow-Up

Discuss your interview with the class. For example, you might discuss which type of reading material most people like. Discuss the differences, if there are any, between what males and females like to read.

Wrap Up

How Much Do You Remember?

Check your new knowledge. In this chapter you learned facts, words, and expressions. You also learned reading skills and you practiced writing. Complete the following to check what you remember.

1. What is *SQ3R?* How does it work? _____

   _____

2. Give two examples of active reading. _____

   _____

3. What are the five parts of the Five-Part Reading System? _____

   _____

4. What's another word for *demanding?* _____

5. What does *auditory learner* mean? _____

   _____

6. What does *form a picture in your mind* mean? _____

   _____

7. When you first go to a webpage, what things should you scan for? _____

   _____

Second Timed Readings

Now reread "I Can't Believe How Much Reading We Have to Do!" and "Active Reading." Time each reading separately. Write your times in the Timed Reading Chart on page 234.

Crossword Puzzle

Complete the crossword puzzle to practice some words and expressions from this chapter.

CLUES

Across ➜

1. Ideas
7. This type of learner needs to move around
9. Like athletes, readers need to _____ _____ before they read.
10. Known to work: _____- _____- _____

Down ⬇

2. Another word for *understand*
3. Say in your own words
4. Feel as though something is impossible
5. If you _____ _____ with the reading, it's easier to understand.
6 To help you remember them, _____ the main ideas out loud.
8. Difficult

CHAPTER **2** Test-Taking Skills

> There are no secrets to success. It is the result of preparation, hard work, learning from failure. 🐦
>
> —*General Colin Powell (Former United States Secretary of State, b. 1937)*

CHAPTER PREVIEW

In this chapter, you'll:

Content
- ▶ learn about six types of tests
- ▶ discover how successful students prepare for tests

Reading Skills
- ▶ prepare for a reading by connecting with the topic
- ▶ identify details in a reading

Vocabulary Skills
- ▶ use words and expressions to talk about types of tests and test-taking strategies
- ▶ use two-word verbs to discuss tests and test-taking

Writing Skills
- ▶ write about test preparation and compare types of test

Internet Skills
- ▶ evaluate search results on the Internet

SHORT SURVEY

The tests that I like best are:
- ❏ true/false tests
- ❏ multiple-choice tests
- ❏ short-answer tests
- ❏ essay tests
- ❏ oral exams (spoken—not written—exams)
- ❏ other _____

Reading 1:
What are six kinds of tests? Read "Types of Tests" to find out.

Reading 2:
How do successful students prepare for tests? Find out in "How to Prepare for a Test."

What do you think?

Answer the questions about your test-taking experiences. Then ask your partner about his or her experiences. Discuss your answers.

Your Test-Taking Experiences

What kinds of test have you taken? Think about tests that you take now and tests that you took in the past. Think about tests in English and in your native language. Circle the answers. For numbers 8 and 9 also fill in the blank.

Note: In an oral exam, you tell the answers to the instructor.

1. In my English language classes, most of the tests are:

    a. true/false   **b.** short-answer   **c.** essay   **d.** oral   **e.** other

2. In my math classes, most of the tests are:

    a. true/false   **b.** short-answer   **c.** essay   **d.** oral   **e.** other

3. In my history classes, most of the tests are:

    a. true/false   **b.** short-answer   **c.** essay   **d.** oral   **e.** other

4. In my science classes, most of the tests are:

    a. true/false   **b.** short-answer   **c.** essay   **d.** oral   **e.** other

5. In my physical education classes, we *do/do not* have tests.
                                    (Circle one)

6. In my art classes, we *do/do not* have tests.
                (Circle one)

7. In my music classes, we *do/do not* have tests.
                   (Circle one)

8. In my _____ classes, most of the tests are:
               (Class)

    a. true/false   **b.** short-answer   **c.** essay   **d.** oral   **e.** other

9. In my _____ classes, we *do/do not* have tests.
               (Class)   (Circle one)

Reading 1: Types of Tests

Before You Read

Preview

A. The title of Reading 1 is "Types of Tests." Pick three of the tests that you talked about on page 27 and discuss them in more detail with a partner. What do they look like? How do you take them?

B. How difficult are different types of tests for you? Read each item in the following box and circle the answer that is true for you. (Note: At the bottom of the page are examples of three kinds of tests.) Share your answers with your partner.

3 = very difficult	2 = somewhat difficult	1 = not difficult		0 = doesn't apply to me
1. Essay tests	3	2	1	0
2. Multiple-choice tests	3	2	1	0
3. Short-answer tests	3	2	1	0
4. Oral tests	3	2	1	0
5. In-class, open-book tests	3	2	1	0
6. Take-home tests	3	2	1	0
7. Other _____	3	2	1	0

C. What strategies do you have for taking each type of test? Share your ideas with your partner.

Short-answer Test

Answer the questions in complete sentences.

1. What is the difference between normal membrane and excitable membrane?

2. Describe the action of troponin and tropomyosin.

In-class, Open-book Test

Answer the following questions. You may use your books and notes.

1. In the first paragraph of the novel, Holden Caulfield rejects the idea that the events he describes in the novel consist of his life story, or that this story is indicative of any larger message. Do you agree or disagree with this statement? Use examples from the book to support your ideas.

Essay Test

We have studied three different aspects of the onset of World War II. Choose two of these aspects and compare and contrast them. You have 30 minutes to complete your essay.

Vocabulary

Here are some words and expressions from "Types of Tests." Match each word or expression with its correct meaning. Write the letter of the correct answer on the line.

Words and Expressions

C **1.** apply

_____ **2.** make a good impression

_____ **3.** incomplete

_____ **4.** mark

_____ **5.** material

_____ **6.** penalized

_____ **7.** statement

Meanings

a. punished

b. information

c. use; make work

d. make others think well of you

e. make a note

f. not complete

g. sentence, fact, or message

As You Read

As you read, think about this question:

▶ How can you prepare for different types of tests?

🎧 Types of Tests

There are six types of tests that teachers like to give: true/false, multiple-choice, short-answer, essay, open book, and oral. Here are some hints for taking each type.

True/false Tests

In a **true/false test,** you read a statement and decide if it's true or not. With true/false tests, every part of the sentence must be true for the answer to be true. Watch out for words like *always, every, none,* and *never.* They are likely to make the answer *false.*

Multiple-choice Tests

In a **multiple-choice test,** there are two parts to the question. The first part is called the stem. The second part has several answer choices. With multiple-choice tests, always find out if you are penalized for guessing. If not, answer every question. First, read the stem and try to answer it without looking at the answer choices. Then read the choices and choose the best one.

Short-answer Tests

In **short-answer tests,** you are asked a question. The answer may be one word, several words, a sentence, or a few sentences. With short-answer tests, pay attention to keywords like *define* and *list;* they tell you what type of answer to give. Give all the answers to the question that seem correct, or speak to the instructor and explain that you can think of more than one right answer. Use short, simple sentences to write your answers.

Essay Tests

For **essay tests,** outline your answers first. Watch how much time you spend on the answers. For example, with 50 minutes to answer four questions, first use ten minutes to outline all four answers, and then take ten minutes to write each answer. Move to the next question when the ten minutes are up, but leave space

5

10

15

20

if you do not finish so you can finish later. Four incomplete answers are usually better than two complete ones.

Open-book Tests

An **open-book test** is one where you can use your textbook during the test. Often you can also use class notes, or your own notes. With open-book tests, you may be asked to apply the material in the book to new situations. Open-book tests can be take-home or classroom tests because there really is no way to cheat. In general, prepare for the test in the same way as you would for a closed-book test. Then mark or jot down notes and any important page numbers that you think you will need. For example, mark the page number for a graph or table that you think the teacher will want you to use.

Oral Exams

When taking **oral exams,** try to make a good impression. Look well rested, not tired. Turn off your cell phone or pager. Stay on topic. If you don't know an answer, tell the teacher how you could find it. Don't give one-word answers. Explain "yes" and "no" answers. Thank the instructor after the exam.

Knowing about an exam before you take it will help you prepare. Of course, the teacher will tell you about an exam several days before you have to take it, and some teachers even ask students to submit sample questions before the exam. This helps students prepare for the exam. If a teacher doesn't do this, write your own questions to help yourself get ready. Guessing what's on an exam is one of the best ways to prepare.

Word Count: 510

Source: *Peak Performances: Success in College and Beyond* (Ferrett)

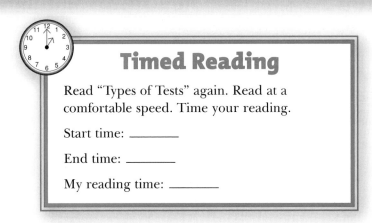

Timed Reading

Read "Types of Tests" again. Read at a comfortable speed. Time your reading.

Start time: _____

End time: _____

My reading time: _____

After You Read

Comprehension

A. Fill in the bubble of the sentence that best describes the main idea of "Types of Tests."

- (A) There are six types of test.
- (B) Knowing about an exam will help you prepare for it.
- (C) For essay tests, outline your answers first.

B. Fill in the bubble for each correct answer.

1. In a true/false test, _____.

   - (A) only part of the sentence must be true
   - (B) the words *always, every, none* and *never* are unimportant
   - (C) every part of the sentence must be true

2. With multiple-choice questions, _____.

   - (A) there are three parts to the question
   - (B) try to answer the stem without looking at the answers
   - (C) you are always penalized for guessing

3. On a short-answer test, the answer cannot be _____.

   - (A) one word
   - (B) several words
   - (C) several paragraphs

4. For essay tests, which is *usually* NOT true?

   - (A) You should outline your answers first.
   - (B) You should fully complete an answer before you move to the next one.
   - (C) You can get credit for an incomplete answer.

5. In an oral exam, you should _____.

   - (A) say nothing if you don't know the answer
   - (B) give one-word answers
   - (C) thank the instructor afterwards

Reading 2: How to Prepare for a Test

Before You Read

Preview

A. The title of Reading 2 is "How to Prepare for a Test." What do you think are some ways to prepare for a test? Discuss your ideas with a partner.

B. Preview these words and expressions from the reading. Complete each sentence below with the correct word or expression.

emphasize	familiar	footnotes	form a group
graph	hints	ignore	require

1. It is important to pay attention to what the instructor says. Never _____ the

   instructor.

2. Teachers give clues about what will be on the test. These _____ can be a big help.

3. Before an exam, get two or three friends together and study with them. If you

   _____ _____ _____, it makes studying easier.

4. If you read a passage twice, the second time the information will be _____.

5. Professor Sanders always tells students what he thinks is important. He tries to

   _____ important points.

6. Some students think that the notes at the bottom of the page or at the end of a chapter are

   not important. However, sometimes teachers ask questions about _____.

7. Some teachers will not allow students to write in pencil. They _____ students to

   write in ink.

8. A _____ or a diagram can be just as important as the words in a textbook passage.

   They show information with pictures and symbols instead of words.

Reading Skills

Connecting with the Topic

Good readers connect with the topic of a reading. They can guess the topic from the reading's title. They think about the topic before they read about it. They ask questions about it, connect their interests and needs to it, and make predictions about it before they read. This helps them to prepare for the reading. Because they are prepared, they can focus better and understand more as they read.

How can you do this? When you look at the topic before you read, first think about what you do and don't already know about it. Ask yourself questions about the topic. Make associations with it and try to find some personal connection to it. Apply your own needs and interests. Think about the topic and try to connect it to people, places, what you like, what you do in your free time, or your subjects in school. Finally, make predictions about the reading.

Here's an example:
Topic: How to read a textbook
Questions: Are there strategies for reading textbooks? Do they make reading textbooks easier? Do they help you to remember the material better?
Interests and Needs: I have a lot of reading this semester. I want to do well in school. I need to keep my grades above a B to keep my financial aid.
Prediction: This passage might tell me how to be a successful reader. It might talk about different reading strategies. It might tell me how to use what I read to pass tests.

Practice

Reading 2 is about preparing for tests. Work with a partner and practice connecting with this topic. Ask questions, think about your interests and needs, and make predictions about the reading. Use the box below or write on a separate piece of paper.

Topic: Preparing for tests	My Questions:	My Partner's Questions:
	My Interests and Needs:	My Partner's Interests and Needs:

Our Prediction:
This passage might be about: _____
_____

As You Read

As you read, think about this question:

▶ What different ways are there to prepare for a test?

🎧 How to Prepare for a Test

Everyone wants to do well on tests. Here are some suggestions from successful students on how to do well on tests.

Throughout the Semester

Listen to the instructor from the first day of class for hints about what is important. For example, the instructor will emphasize the important information by repeating it or telling you it is important. When you review your textbook and notes, you should already know what is important. After each lecture, review your notes. Come to class ready to ask questions about what you don't understand.

Look at the visual aids the instructor uses. For example, if the instructor asks you to look at a diagram or graph in your textbook, make sure you understand why that diagram or graph is important. There may be a question on the test that asks about that diagram.

Study for an essay exam. Students who prepare for essay exams do better on all types of exams. Essay exams require students to know more information than is required for multiple-choice, true/false, or short-answer exams. There are no hints on the exam itself, so students must learn more for essay exams.

To prepare for an essay exam, always read the material twice before you start taking notes. When you read the material the first time, it may seem difficult. When you read the material the second time, it will seem familiar. This is similar to when you have to find the way to a friend's house for the first time. The second time you go to your friend's house, it's easier because you know the way. It may even seem shorter because you don't have to slow down as much to check street names or landmarks. The same is true with the material you read. The second time the words and ideas will be familiar.

After you've read the material two times, take notes. At this point, you'll find that you know some of the material and can focus on what is most important. Don't ignore footnotes in your reading. Sometimes instructors think the information in a footnote is important and will ask a question about it. Write down the important information in your notes. After you take notes, go back and add your opinions to them. Note the ideas that you agree with and the ideas that you disagree with. People retain information better when they have opinions about it.

30 **Write** down your own test questions and answer them. Pretend that you are the teacher. What do you want your students to know?

Work with a friend. You can study together in many ways. For instance, you and your friend can spend about ten minutes writing questions (use some of the questions that you wrote for yourself) then exchange papers and answer

35 the questions. Did you and your friend ask similar questions? If you both wrote down the same question, maybe the instructor will ask it, too.

Form a study group. After studying with a friend, you will have a lot to contribute to the study group, and you

40 will also learn from them. For example, you will see some points you missed when you were studying earlier. Talking about the material with others will help you remember it better.

A Study Group

Before the Exam

Think positive thoughts about yourself and about the exam. For example, tell your-

45 self that you will do your best. Tell yourself that you will read all the questions before you start. Also, remind yourself to answer the questions that you know first, and then answer the others.

Get enough sleep the night before the exam. Some students have nightmares about missing an exam because the alarm didn't go off or they were too sleepy to get up. It's not just a nightmare. Some students actually do

50 sleep through exams!

Go to the room early so that you will be relaxed and comfortable by the time the instructor passes out the exam.

Bring a good luck charm to the exam. It may not help, but it can't hurt.

A Good Luck Charm

Word Count:. 679

Source: *Peak Performances: Successs in College and Beyond* (Ferrett)

Timed Reading

Read "How to Prepare for a Test" again. Read at a comfortable speed. Time your reading.

Start time: _____

End time: _____

My reading time: _____

After You Read

Main Idea

Which sentence best describes the main idea of "How to Prepare for a Test"? Fill in the bubble of the best answer.

(A) To prepare well for an exam, you must prepare throughout the term and right before the exam.

(B) To prepare well for an exam, you must read the material twice and take notes.

(C) To prepare well for an exam, you must have a positive attitude.

Reading Skills

Identifying Details

When you read, it's important to get the main ideas in a passage. It is also important to find and understand the details since these are often the answers to test questions. Details support and explain main ideas. You often find them in sentences that contain examples. Details also explain words and ideas. The writer often gives hints to help you identify these details. Hints include expressions that introduce examples (*for example, such as, for instance*). Hints can also be keywords repeated from main idea statements.

Examples:
Main Idea: When you read, look at the visual aids. (*Reader Question:* What visual aids should I look at?) ➡ *Detail:* **For example,** if the instructor asks you to look at a diagram or graph in your textbook, make sure you understand why that diagram or graph is important. *Hint:* **For example**

Main Idea: To prepare for any test, always study for an **essay exam.** (*Reader Question:* Why should I study for an essay exam?) ➡ *Detail:* **Essay exams** require students to know more information than is required for multiple-choice, true/false, or short-answer exams. *Hint:* Key words are repeated: **essay exam** and **essay exams.**

Getting the Details

A. Find the details needed to answer these questions. Look for examples and explanations in "How to Prepare for a Test." Look for clues such as *for example* and repeating keywords.

1. How does an instructor give hints about what is important? _____

_____

2. Why should you read material twice to prepare for an exam? (Hint: Look for the keyword

familiar.) _____

_____

3. Why should you add your opinions to test preparation notes? _____

_____

4. What is one way to study with a friend? _____

_____

5. How can a study group help you prepare for a test? _____

_____

6. What is an example of a *positive thought*? _____

_____

Talk About It

Discuss these questions in small groups.

1. Which test preparation techniques that you read about were new to you?

2. Do you ever have dreams (nightmares or good dreams) about school or about test-taking? If yes, describe one of your dreams.

3. Do tests make you nervous? If yes, what do you do to stop feeling nervous?

4. Do you have trouble sleeping before tests? If yes, what do you do to sleep better?

B. Look at the list of test-taking strategies from "How to Prepare for a Test." Put each of them in the correct category: Strategies for Throughout the Term or Strategies for Before the Exam.

> **Test-Taking Strategies**
> Bring a good luck charm to the exam.
> Form a discussion group.
> Get enough sleep the night before the exam.
> Go to the exam room early.
> Listen to the instructor for hints about what is important.
> Look at the visual aids the instructor uses.
> Study for an essay exam.
> Think positive thoughts.
> Work with a friend.
> Write your own questions and answer them.

Strategies for Throughout the Term	Strategies for Before the Exam

Vocabulary

A. Here are some more words and expressions from "How to Prepare for a Test." Find them in the reading and circle them.

Nouns		Verbs
good luck charm study group	landmarks nightmare	exchange pretend remind

B. Now use them to complete the sentences.

1. To prepare for an exam, try to imagine that you are the teacher. If you _____ that you are the teacher, you will understand what the teacher wants you to know.

2. For luck, Mary carries a small metal horseshoe on her key chain. She brings this _____ _____ _____ with her to all her exams.

3. Teachers sometimes want students to correct each other's work, so they ask students to _____ papers with a partner.

4. To remember where a friend lives, you may look for a post office on the corner or a school with a big tree in front of it near your friend's house. These _____ can be very helpful.

5. In the reading, you learned to answer the questions that you know first. _____ yourself of this strategy before you take a test.

6. Students who work together find this practice helps them do well. A _____ _____ can be very helpful.

7. Pat had a bad dream before the exam. He had a _____ that his alarm didn't go off and he missed the exam.

Expressions

Two-Word Verbs for Talking about Tests and Test-Taking

Two-word verbs are expressions with a verb and one or more prepositions. You can use them to talk about tests.

Here are some two-word verb expressions from Reading 1 and Reading 2 used to discuss tests and test-taking:

agree with   contribute to   find out   focus on   prepare for   watch out for

Example:

Students who prepare for essay exams do better on all types of tests.

Practice

A. Find and underline the two-word verb expressions from the box in "Types of Tests" or "How to Prepare for a Test."

B. Now use some of them to complete the sentences.

1. The teacher will spend a lot of time on the important points. Students should

   _____ _____ those points, too.

2. Talk to your study group about what you are studying. When you

   _____ _____ a study group, it helps you remember information for the test.

3. On true/false tests, it's important to look for words such as *always, every, none,* or

   never. _____ _____ _____ these words because

   they can make the answer false.

4. If you don't know when the test will be, you can _____

   _____ by asking the instructor.

5. Analyze the ideas in a passage to decide if you _____ _____
   them or disagree with them. Giving your opinion makes you an active reader
   and helps you remember the material.

Internet Research

Evaluating URLs in Search Results

When you do an Internet search, you often get thousands of results. Some of these web-pages may have correct and accurate information. Others may have incorrect or false information. How can you tell? For starters, you can look carefully at the Universal Resource Locator (URL—the website address) for each result. URL endings tell you the person or organization that is responsible for the site. These endings include:

.com   .edu   .gov   .org

The ending ".com" usually means the site is for a store or a business. The ending ".edu" is for an educational institution, such as a college or university. The ending ".gov" is used by government agencies, and ".org" is for nonprofit organizations such as charities.

Read the URL to decide if the website has the information you want. For example, imagine that you want to get information about taking tests. You might find these URLs in your results:

http://www.sas.calpoly.edu/asc/ssl/tests.general.html
http://www.princetonreview.com/

Which site should you look at first? Probably the first site because it has an ".edu," and universities such as Cal Poly help students study. The Princeton Review source probably has information about tests, but you may have to buy it.

Hint: Even if a source has in the URL the name of a university, such as Princeton, it is not from the actual university unless it includes ".edu."

Practice

To practice evaluating URLs, follow these steps.

- ▶ Do a search for "taking essay tests" or "improving test scores."
- ▶ Look at the URLs on the first page of your results.
- ▶ Pick one or two results that you think will have good information.
- ▶ Go to the websites and check them out. Were you right? Look at some websites that you think come from a business. (These are often on the right-hand side of the page.) Were you right?
- ▶ If you can, print your search results page. Circle the useful URLs and underline the ones that weren't useful.
- ▶ Bring the page to class and discuss your experience.

Write About It

A. Write the following paragraphs. Fill in the blanks. Write complete sentences.

Paragraph One

It's a good idea to prepare for tests both throughout the term and just before an exam.

Throughout the term, you should _____
(Explain one thing you should do throughout the term)

_____.

You should also _____
(Explain another thing you should do throughout the term)

_____.

Before an exam, it's a good idea to _____
(Describe one thing you should do before the exam)

_____.

and _____
(Describe another thing that you should do before the exam)

_____.

These things are helpful because _____
(Give one reason why these things help you to be successful)

_____.

Paragraph Two

Some types of exams are easy and others are hard. In my opinion, the most difficult type of

exam is the/a _____. It's difficult because
(Give the name of a type of exam that you think is difficult. Use the singular form)

_____.
(Explain why it's difficult for you)

For example, _____.
(Give a specific example of why it's difficult)

On the other hand, I think that _____ are

(Give the name of a type of exam that is easy for you; use the plural form)

easy because _____.

(Explain why this type is easy for you)

For instance, _____.

(Give a specific example of why this type is easy)

B. Now write your own paragraphs. Write one paragraph about preparing for tests and another about tests that are easy and those that are hard. Try to include words and expressions from this chapter in your paragraphs.

C. Write more paragraphs about tests and taking tests. Use five words and expressions from this chapter and your Internet research. Choose from the following topics.

▶ Describe how you feel about taking tests. What kind of tests do you like? Why? What kinds do you dislike? Why?

▶ Describe the last test that you took. What kind of test was it? How did you prepare? How did you do? In what ways could you prepare better next time?

▶ Give advice to a friend on how to prepare for an exam.

▶ Compare two tests that you took. In what classes or situations did you take the tests? How were they similar? How were they different? How did you do?

▶ Use your own idea.

On Your Own

Project

Take a survey. Ask your classmates about their favorite types of tests.

Step 1: Practice

Listen as your teacher reads the survey question ("What's your favorite type of test?") and the test types. Repeat them with your teacher so you can pronounce them correctly.

Step 2: Take a Survey

Ask five students about their favorite types of tests. Check (✓) the box of their favorite type of test. Then write why that type of test is their favorite.

What's Your Favorite Type of Test?						
Type of Test	Student Answers					
	Student 1	Student 2	Student 3	Student 4	Student 5	Why?
True/false						
Short-answer						
Multiple-choice						
Essay						
In-class open-book						
Take-home exam						

Step 3: Follow-Up

Explain the results of your survey to the class. Also, discuss which types of tests most people like and why.

Wrap Up

How Much Do You Remember?

Check your new knowledge. In this chapter, you learned facts, words, and expressions. You also learned reading skills and you practiced writing. Complete the following to check what you remember.

1. What are six types of tests? _____

   _____

2. What is the easiest type of test for you to study for? _____

   Why? _____

   _____

3. Write three things to do throughout the term to prepare for a test. _____

   _____

4. Write two things that you can do to prepare just before a test. _____

   _____

5. Use *incomplete* in a sentence. _____

   _____

6. Use *watch out for* in a sentence. _____

   _____

7. How can you evaluate a website before you go to it? _____

   _____

Second Timed Readings

Now reread "Types of Tests" and "How to Prepare for a Test." Time each reading separately. Write your times in the Timed Reading Chart on page 234.

Crossword Puzzle

Complete the crossword puzzle to practice some words and expressions from this chapter.

CLUES

Across →

1. Discover

5. The small notes at the bottom of a page

6. Essay exams _____ students to know more information than other types of exams.

8. A bad dream

9. A clue

Down ↓

1. Put people into a group

2. Not pay attention to

3. Speak up (in a group)

4. The opposite of *disagree with*

7. Say or read aloud

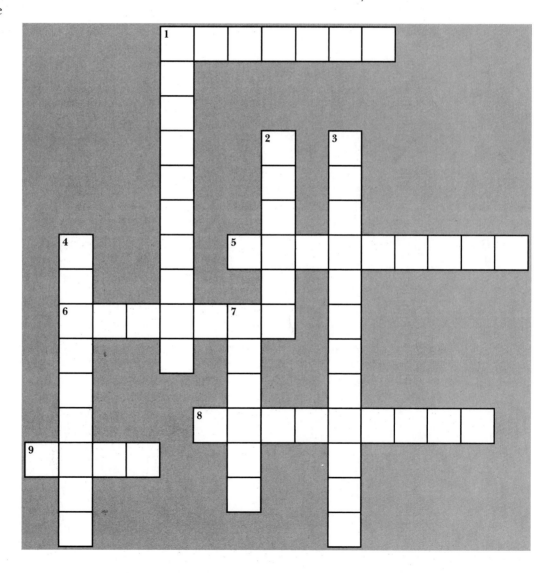

What is History?

History is the record of events from the past to the present. Historians study ancient times through modern times. Some historians focus on economics, politics, science, or medicine. Others focus on art, music, or language. Some areas of history that historians study are:

- the Meiji period in Japan
- the Aztec and Mayan Empires
- the history of religions
- the history of dance
- the development of technology

One of the first historians was Herodotus of Halicarnassus (c.485–c.429 B.C.). He wrote a book about the wars between the Persians and the Greeks called *The Histories*, published between 430 and 424 B.C.

SOME FAMOUS HISTORIANS

Sima Qian—Chinese, 145–c.90 B.C.

Marcus Tullius Cicero—Roman, c.106–3 B.C.

Anna Comnena—Byzantine, 1083–1153

Thomas Carlyle—Scots English, 1795–1881

Leopold von Ramke—German, 1795–1866

Jules Michelet—French, 1798–1874

Jacques Barzun—French American, 1907–

Lee Gi-Baek—Korean, 1924–2004

Yuji Ichioka—Japanese American, 1936–2002

History and You

People who study history work in education, business, and publishing. They work as researchers, teachers, advisors, writers, editors, and lawyers.

Do you want to study history? Ask yourself these questions:

- Am I curious about the past?
- Do I want to study one period of time or topic in depth?
- Do I want to research what happened in the past to understand today's world?
- Am I interested in different countries and cultures?

CHAPTER 3

World History: 1000-1500 A.D.

CHAPTER PREVIEW

In this chapter, you'll:

Content
▶ read a travel journal written in the 1300s
▶ learn about cross-cultural exchange in Asia, the Middle East, and Europe from 1000 to 1500 A.D.

Reading Skills
▶ preview a reading by asking questions about the title and headings
▶ identify examples used to illustrate ideas

Vocabulary Skills
▶ use words and expressions to talk about trade and travel in the past
▶ use travel expressions to talk about traveling over time and places

Writing Skills
▶ write about cross-cultural exchanges in history and about favorite historical periods

Internet Skills
▶ use the Internet to find biographies of famous people in history

> History repeats itself. ❧
>
> —*Anonymous*

SHORT SURVEY

I like to read about the history of:

❏ the whole world

❏ my country/culture

❏ another country/culture

❏ the lives of important people

❏ science, technology, or art

❏ other _____

Reading 1:

What did a 14th-century Moroccan discover as he traveled to China? Read Ibn Battuta's travel journal to find out.

Reading 2:

What new ideas and products did people learn about from 1000 to 1500 A.D.? "Cross-Cultural Exchange: 1000–1500 A.D." has some answers.

What do you think?

Here are some important inventions and discoveries throughout history. Which one happened first? Put the items in chronological order using 1 for the earliest and 8 for the most recent.

History Quiz: What Happened First?

_____ writing

_____ paper money

_____ the wheel

_____ paper

_____ the printing press

_____ gunpowder

_____ metal swords

_____ ink

---

1. the wheel: Sumeria, 3500 B.C.*
2. writing: Sumeria, 3500 to 3000 B.C.
3. ink: Egypt, 3000 B.C.
4. metal swords: the Middle East, 2000 B.C.
5. gunpowder: China, 187 B.C.
6. paper (as we know it today): China, 1 A.D.**
7. paper money, China, 1023 A.D.
8. the printing press: Europe, 1450 A.D.

Note: Dates are approximate.

*B.C. refers to dates before the Year 1 in the Western calendar.

**A.D. includes dates from Year 1 to the present in the Western calendar.

Now compare your answers with a partner and discuss these questions.

1. How close to the correct order are your answers? (See box above.)
2. Were you surprised by the order of any of the events? Why or why not?
3. Do you know anything else about these events? For example, do you know where they happened?

I thought paper money was before gunpowder.

I knew that one.

Reading 1: Ibn Battuta: Long-Distance Traveler

Before You Read

Preview

A. The title of Reading 1 is "Ibn Battuta: Long-Distance Traveler." Ibn Battuta was born in North Africa in 1304 A.D. What do you think life was like in Battuta's time? How did people live? What did they know about the world? What kinds of technology did they have? Discuss your ideas with a partner.

B. Ibn Battuta traveled for almost 30 years throughout Africa, the Middle East, and China. The map below shows many of the countries Ibn Battuta visited. Work with a partner. Tell your partner what you know about each country. (Note: Only some of the countries that Battuta visited are labeled on the map.)

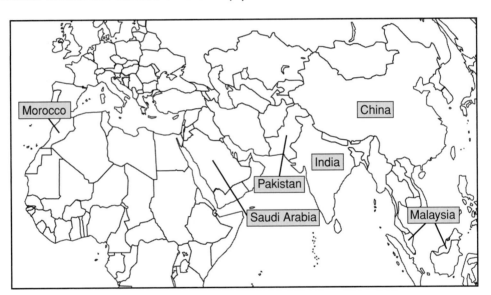

Vocabulary

A. Here are some words and expressions from "Ibn Battuta: Long-Distance Traveler." Match each word or expression with its correct meaning. Write the letter of the correct answer on the line.

Words and Expressions

_____ **1.** state (such as Morocco)

_____ **2.** resembles

_____ **3.** fiber

_____ **4.** channel

_____ **5.** marveled at

_____ **6.** manes

_____ **7.** bank

_____ **8.** be accompanied by

_____ **9.** takes on

_____ **10.** flows out of

Meanings

a. was amazed by

b. be with; go with

c. land on the side of a river

d. string; thread

e. comes out of

f. a narrow body of water

g. looks like

h. has; gets

i. country

j. long hair on the back of horses' heads and necks

B. Battuta's journal was written in the 1300s and is translated from Arabic, so some words and expressions in his journal sound poetic or old-fashioned. Match each of these poetic words or expressions with its correct meaning.

Poetic Words or Expressions

_____ **1.** beasts

_____ **2.** taking (them) to be

_____ **3.** bind

Meanings

a. believing that they were

b. join; connect

c. animals

As You Read

As you read, think about this question:

▶ What did Battuta find strange or unusual
   on his journeys (trips)?

🎧 Ibn Battuta: Long-Distance Traveler

Abu Abdullah Muhammad Ibn Battuta was born in Tangier, Morocco in 1304 A.D. At the age of 20, Battuta left northern Africa and traveled for almost 30 years throughout Africa, the Middle East, and China. He visited every Muslim state that existed at the time. After traveling over 70,000 miles, he came back to Morocco and recorded his journeys. The following are parts of his travel journal. They focus on some of the things that Battuta found new and strange.

Coconut Trees in Yemen

The coco palm is one of the strangest of trees and looks exactly like a date palm. The nut resembles a man's head; it has marks like eyes and a mouth, and the contents, when it is green, are like the brain. It has fiber like hair, out of which they (*the Yemenis*) make ropes, which they use instead of nails to bind their ships together.

Something strange is that oil (*and*) milk...are taken from it. The milk is made by putting the contents of the nut in water, which takes on the color and taste of milk and is used

Coconuts and Coco Palm

along with food. To make the oil, the ripe nuts are peeled and the contents dried in the sun, then cooked in pots and the oil taken out. They use it for lighting and dip bread in it, and the women put it on their hair.

A Hippopotamus

The Hippopotamus of the River Niger

I was accompanied by a merchant called Abu Bakr ibn Ya'qub. We took the Mima road... We came to a wide channel, which flows out of the Niger and can only be crossed in boats... On reaching it, I saw sixteen beasts with enormous bodies, and marveled at them, taking them to be elephants, of which there are many in that country.

25

Afterwards I saw that they had gone into the river, so I said to Abu Bakr, "What kind of animals are these?" He replied, "They are hippopotami (plural of hippopotamus) that have come out to eat." They are bigger than horses, have manes and tails, and their heads are like horses' heads, but their feet like elephants' feet. I saw these hippopotami again when we sailed down the Niger from Timbuktu to Gawgaw. They were swimming in the water, and lifting their heads and blowing. The men in the boat were afraid of them and kept close to the bank in case the hippopotami should sink them.

30

Although he is not as well known as another long-distance traveler, Marco Polo, Ibn Battuta is remembered today. There are many books about him, and a crater on the moon is named after him.

Word Count:. 442

Source: *Travels in Asia and Africa 1325–1354*, (Battuta; tr. and ed. Gibb.)

Timed Reading

Read "Ibn Battuta: Long-Distance Traveler" again. Read at a comfortable speed. Time your reading.

Start time: _____

End time: _____

My reading time: _____ minutes

Years, Centuries, and Ages

Middle Ages
1000s–11th century
1100s–12th century
1200s–13th century
1300s–14th century

Renaissance
1400s–15th century
1500s–16th century

Age of Revolution
1600s–17th century
1700s–18th century

Modern Age
1800s–19th century
1900s–20th century
2000s–21st century

After You Read

Comprehension

A. Fill in the bubble of the sentence that best describes the main idea of "Ibn Battuta: Long-Distance Traveler."

    (A) Ibn Battuta discovered coconuts in Yemen during the 14th century.

    (B) Ibn Battuta was a long-distance traveler during the 14th century.

    (C) Ibn Battuta traveled 70,000 miles during the 14th century.

B. Fill in the bubble for each correct answer.

1. Which of the following is NOT a use of the coconut, according to Battuta?

    (A) in lighting   (B) to make ropes   (C) to make nails

2. Which statement is probably true?

    (A) Battuta saw elephants in a channel of the Niger River.

    (B) Battuta thought that he saw elephants in a channel of the Niger River.

    (C) Battuta saw both elephants and hippos in a channel of the Niger River.

3. Which statement is true?

    (A) Battuta traveled down the Niger River to Gawgaw in a boat.

    (B) Battuta traveled along the Niger River to Gawgaw on horseback.

    (C) Battuta traveled along the Niger River to Gawgaw on foot.

4. Which statement is true, according to the passage?

    (A) Ibn Battuta is better known than Marco Polo.

    (B) Ibn Battuta is not as well known as Marco Polo.

    (C) Ibn Battuta and Marco Polo were the same person.

Talk About It

Discuss the following question with a partner.

What are some reasons for studying history?

Reading 2: Cross-Cultural Exchange: 1000–1500 A.D.

Before You Read

Reading Skills

Using the Title and Headings to Preview

You can preview the main ideas of a reading passage by reading its title and any headings that divide the passage into sections. The title often gives hints about the main idea, and the headings often tell you the supporting ideas.

Before you read, scan the title and the headings of a passage. Ask yourself questions about them. Then make guesses about the passage. For example, look at the title of Reading 1 in Chapter 2:

Title: "Types of Tests"
Possible Questions: What are some types of tests? Does knowing about test types make you a better test-taker?
Headings: True/False Tests, Multiple-choice Tests, Short-answer, Essay Tests, Open-book Tests, Oral Exams
Questions: What are these tests like?
Possible Guesses about the Passage: This passage describes six test types. It probably explains how to do well on each type.

Thinking about the title and the headings before you read helps you prepare for the reading. It makes the reading easier to understand.

Practice

Preview the title and the headings for Reading 2 on pages 59–61. Use the information to fill in the following chart. Work with a partner.

Headings in Reading 2	Questions about the Headings
1: _____	1: _____
2: _____	2: _____
3: _____	3: _____

Guesses about Reading 2: _____

_____

_____

Preview

Preview these words and expressions from the reading. Complete each of the sentences below with the correct word or expression.

commodities	consulted with	cross-cultural exchange	empire
precious stones	primitive	silk routes	technological benefit

1. Centuries ago, roads went through the Middle East and connected Asia and Europe. Because people used these roads to carry silk from Asia, they were called "_____ _____."

2. Travelers also used the routes between Asia and Europe to move _____ _____ such as sapphires, rubies, and jade.

3. Ancient Egypt used a very _____ kind of paper called *papyrus;* the Chinese invented a more modern type around 1 A.D.

4. European, Muslim, and Jewish scientists _____ _____ each other in the Middle Ages; these discussions led to many new ideas and inventions.

5. The Mongols once ruled an enormous area of land. Their _____ included the modern countries of Mongolia, Russia, and China.

6. Long-distance travel during the years from 1000 to 1500 A.D. led to many useful ideas and inventions. One _____ _____ was the magnetic compass.

7. Africans learned about new fruits from Muslims; Europeans got noodles from the Chinese. This _____ - _____ _____ improved the lives of many people.

Magnetic Compass

8. Travelers could not carry heavy _____ such as wood and large stones, so they moved these products on ships.

As You Read

As you read, think about this question:
▶ What were some of the benefits (positive results) of long-distance travel between Asia, the Middle East, and Europe?

🎧 Cross-Cultural Exchange: 1000–1500 A.D.

Today, we are connected to people all over the world by air routes, boats, phone lines, trains, and the Internet. We can easily communicate with people in distant lands by phone or email; we can buy foreign products with the click of a button. However, it may be surprising to note that in some parts of the world, the
5 period over 500 years ago from 1000 to 1500 A.D., was also a time of extensive long-distance travel, cross-cultural exchange, and international trading activity.

An Age of Travel

From 1000 to 1500 A.D., people in the eastern hemisphere traveled, traded, communicated, and interacted more regularly and intensively than ever before. One of the reasons they traveled great distances over land and sea was to trade
10 goods. Merchants (people who bought and sold things) traveled by land to trade silk, spices, and precious stones. They traveled over the silk routes that ran from Europe through Central Asia to China. They also traveled by sea over the Indian Ocean and the South China Sea to move heavier commodities such as wood, stones, and other building materials.

Marco Polo

15 One of the most famous long-distance travelers of this time was Marco Polo. Marco Polo was Italian. He, his father, and uncle were the first European merchants to visit China. They traveled from Venice through Armenia, Persia, and Afghanistan, and all along the silk routes to China.

20 Polo's reports of his journeys contain fascinating details about the places he saw and the people he met. For example, in his writings he describes the Mongols, a group of people who lived in what are now Mongolia, Russia, and China. The Mongols were a powerful people who controlled the largest

Marco Polo

empire in world history. Polo describes their everyday lives, and in particular, their household customs and family structure. He is especially surprised that Mongol women do most of the work. As he writes in his travel journals: "The men do not bother themselves about anything but hunting and warfare and falconry." (Falconry is hunting with birds.)

Although many people did not believe Polo's incredible stories, many historians agree that he probably brought noodles—a major part of the modern Italian diet—to Italy from China.

Cross-Cultural Exchange

As the accounts of Polo and other travelers reveal, the period from 1000 to 1500 was a time of extensive cross-cultural exchange. The movement of products from distant places was one result of this activity. Through travel, people discovered new foods and plants. When travelers brought things to new places, these products often contributed to the region's health, daily life, and economy. One example of this phenomenon was seen in sub-Saharan Africa (the part of Africa that is south of the Sahara Desert). Before 1000 A.D., sub-Saharan Africans did not grow citrus fruits (oranges, lemons, and grapefruits) or cotton. Muslim travelers introduced (brought) citrus to sub-Saharan Africa, which greatly improved the diet of West Africa. Muslims also introduced cotton to West Africa, which grew very well there and became an important part of the economy.

However, merchants and travelers in the eastern hemisphere did more than trade goods. They also exchanged songs, stories, religious and philosophical ideas, and scientific concepts. For instance, the poetry, music, and love songs of Muslim performers influenced the troubadours (traveling musicians) of Europe. Similarly, European scientists consulted with Muslim and Jewish scientists in Sicily and Spain.

Many technological benefits resulted from cross-cultural interaction. One example of this was the magnetic compass. Invented in China around 900 A.D., the magnetic compass spread across the Indian Ocean and reached Europe by the mid-12th century. Soon it was used throughout the Mediterranean and the Atlantic. Before that, sailing was dangerous; with the compass, sailors could travel more safely and cover greater distances than before.

Refined sugar is another example of the technological benefits of cross-cultural exchange. Muslims developed the technology for creating crystallized sugar. Europeans discovered it during their travels in the Middle East and brought the

Crystallized Sugar

technology back to Europe. Before that, Europeans used only honey or fruit as a sweetener.

60

The Mongols were responsible for spreading gunpowder westward. They learned about it from the Chinese. As the Chinese invaded lands in the Middle East, they used catapults to launch (send) gunpowder bombs into cities. Muslims copied this technology in order to fight back. By 1258, gunpowder had reached Europe, and by the early 14th century armies from Europe to China used primitive cannons.

65

The great amount of cross-cultural exchange that happened during this time brought about important changes in the lives of the people of the eastern hemisphere. This exchange improved economies, increased the varieties of food people ate, influenced the songs they sang and the art they created, and changed the nature of warfare forever.

70

Catapult

A Primitive Cannon

Word Count: 756

Source: *Traditions and Encounters: A Global Perspective on the Past* (Bentley and Ziegler)

Timed Reading

Read "Cross-Cultural Exchange: 1000–1500 A.D." again. Read at a comfortable speed. Time your reading.

Start time: _____

End time: _____

My reading time: _____

After You Read

Main Idea

Which sentence best describes the main idea of "Cross-Cultural Exchange: 1000–1500 A.D."? Fill in the bubble of the best answer.

Ⓐ Between 1000–1500, Muslims developed the technology for making refined sugar.

Ⓑ Between 1000–1500, Marco Polo traveled from Italy to Asia.

Ⓒ Between 1000–1500, there was a great deal of travel and cultural exchange.

Reading Skills

Identifying Examples

You saw how to identify details on page 37 in Chapter 2. Examples are one type of detail. Good writers give you examples to help you understand their ideas and to explain or prove them. Following are some expressions that introduce examples:

for example	such as
an/one example is	for instance
X is an example of	

Practice

A. Find and circle the example expressions from the box above in "Cross-Cultural Exchange: 1000–1500 A.D."

B. Now use the examples to answer each of the following questions. There may be more than one answer for some questions.

1. What commodities were moved by sea? _____

_____

2. Which group of people did Polo meet and describe? _____

_____

3. What did merchants and travelers exchange in addition to products? _____

_____

4. What technological benefits resulted from cross-cultural exchange during the period from

1000 to 1500 A.D.? _____

_____

5. What region saw life improve because travelers brought new products into it?_____

_____

Vocabulary

A. Here are some more words and expressions from "Cross-Cultural Exchange: 1000–1500 A.D."
Find them in the reading and circle them.

Verbs	Adjective
are connected to brought about ran from . . . to reveal spread across	extensive

B. Now use them to complete the sentences.

1. There was a lot of cross-cultural exchange during the Middle Ages. This

_____ exchange of ideas and products improved people's lives.

2. Ideas traveled great distances in the Middle Ages. For example, the idea of the magnetic

compass started in China. It _____ _____ the Middle East

and then went to Europe.

3. Today, many people _____ _____ _____ each

other through email.

4. Ibn Battuta's journals _____ a lot about the kind of person he was. They show

that he was brave, open-minded, and kind.

5. The silk routes _____ _____ Europe _____

China, across the Middle East.

6. Cross-cultural exchange in the Middle Ages caused a lot of changes in the world. For

instance, it _____ _____ new technologies that made sailing safer.

Talk About It

Discuss these questions in small groups.

1. What foreign countries have you visited? What new things (e.g., food, products, ideas) did you discover while you were there?

2. What is the greatest distance you have traveled? How did you travel this distance? (by plane, by car, etc.) Why did you go? What did you bring home? Do you think you will go there again?

Expressions

> ## Expressions with *Travel*
>
> Reading 1 and Reading 2 use many expressions with *travel* plus a preposition. These expressions describe travel over time and place, and by means of transportation.
>
> **Examples;**
> **travel for (time):** Battuta traveled for 20 years.
> **travel along (road/route/river/sea):** Polo traveled along the silk routes.
> **travel by (means of transportation):** Battuta traveled by boat/sea.
> **travel from (place) to (specific place)/through (region):** Polo traveled from Italy to China/through Asia.

Practice

A. Find and underline these *travel* + preposition expressions in "Ibn Battuta: Long-Distance Traveler" or "Cross-Cultural Exchange: 1000–1500 A.D."

B. Now use them to complete the sentences. (Note: There might be more than one correct expression for some sentences.)

1. This summer, Tony and his friends want to _____ _____

   San Diego _____ San Francisco.

2. They plan to _____ _____ car because it's less expensive than

   a plane.

3. Tony and his friends will _____ _____ Highway 1 because it's

   the most interesting route.

4. Ashley plans to take a break after she graduates. She wants to _____

   _____ one year in Europe.

5. One thing that Ashley wants to do in Europe is _____ _____

   Eastern Europe.

Internet Research

Finding Biographies on the Internet

The Internet is a great place to find biographical information about famous people in history. Finding biographies is easy. Just go to a search engine such as Google (www.google.com) and type the name of the person into the text box along with the word *biography*.

Example:

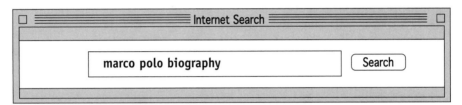

Remember to look carefully at the URLs in the search results—they can tell you a lot about the sources of the information. You can also go to websites that specialize in biographies, such as www.biography.com.

Note: You don't have to use capital letters or punctuation in a search.

Practice

Find on the Internet a few different biographies of a famous person in history. Use one of the people in the Keywords box below or your favorite person in history. Print the best example and bring it to class.

Keywords		
Marco Polo	Leonardo da Vinci	Timur Lenk (Tamerlane)
Genghis Khan	Ibn Battuta	Lady Shikibu Murasaki
Hildegard of Bingen	Attila	Vasco da Gama
Kublai Khan	Leonardo da Vinci	

Discuss your search with the class. What keywords did you use? Did a URL help you choose the best result? Then tell the class about the person you researched.

Write About It

A. Write the following paragraphs. Fill in the blanks. Write complete sentences.

Paragraph One

Long distance travelers during the period from 1000 to 1500 exchanged many things. One thing that they exchanged was _____. For example,
(List one type of thing)

_____.
(Give a specific example of the type)

Another thing that long-distance travelers exchanged was _____.
(List another type of thing)

For instance, _____
(Give a specific example of the type)

_____. Long-distance travelers
(Give a specific example of the type)

also traded _____. An example of this is _____.
(List another type of thing)

_____.
(Give a specific example of the type)

Paragraph Two

My favorite time in history is _____. It's my favorite because
(Give your favorite time period by era or years)

_____.
(Give one reason why it's your favorite)

For example, _____
(Give a specific example)

_____.

It's also my favorite period because _____
(Give another reason why it's your favorite)

For instance, _____
(Give a specific example)

_____.

B. Now write your own paragraphs. Write one paragraph about the things that long-distance travelers exchanged, and another about your favorite period in history. Try to include words and expressions from this chapter in your paragraphs.

C. Write more paragraphs about history. Use five words and expressions from this chapter and your Internet research. Choose from the following topics.

▶ Describe how the world changed in a certain time period.

▶ Write about a famous person from the past.

▶ Explain how a technological invention or discovery changed the world.

▶ Discuss why or why not it's important to study history.

▶ Use your own idea.

> **We must be the authors of the history of our age.**
>
> —*Madeleine Albright (Former American Secretary of State, b.1937)*

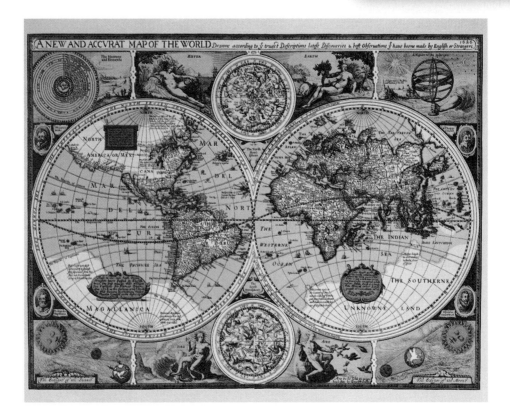

On Your Own

Project

Take a survey. Ask your classmates about their favorite person in history.

Step 1: Practice

Listen as your teacher reads the survey questions. Do you understand them? Repeat the questions with your teacher so you can pronounce them correctly.

Step 2: Take a Survey

Ask three classmates about their favorite person in history. Fill in the chart below.

Favorite Person in History Survey

Person 1: _____

1. Who is your favorite person in history?

    Answer: _____

2. Why is this person your favorite?

    Answer: _____

Person 2: _____

1. Who is your favorite person in history?

    Answer: _____

2. Why is this person your favorite?

    Answer: _____

Person 3: _____

1. Who is your favorite person in history?

    Answer: _____

2. Why is this person your favorite?

    Answer: _____

Step 3: Follow-Up

Explain the results of your survey to the class.

Wrap Up

How Much Do You Remember?

Check your new knowledge. In this chapter you learned facts, words, and expressions. You also learned reading skills and you practiced writing. Complete the following to check what you remember.

1. What two things did Ibn Battuta find surprising on his travels? _____

   _____

2. Name three things that resulted from cross-cultural exchange from 1000 to 1500 A.D.

   _____

3. How can reading the title and the headings of a passage *before* you read the passage itself help

   you? _____

   _____

4. Give two expressions that introduce examples in a passage. _____

   _____

5. Use *technological benefit* in a sentence. _____

   _____

6. Complete this sentence: Ibn Battuta *traveled along* _____.

7. How can you find a biography on the Internet? _____

   _____

Second Timed Readings

Now reread "Ibn Battuta: Long-Distance Traveler" and "Cross-Cultural Exchange: 1000–1500 A.D." Time each reading separately. Write your times in the Timed Reading Chart on page 235.

Crossword Puzzle

Complete the crossword puzzle to practice some words and expressions from this chapter.

CLUES

Across →

1. Not modern
6. Things that are for sale or for trade
7. Ibn Battuta _____ by boat.
8. Looks like
9. Another word for *exchanging*

Down ↓

2. The magnetic compass was one of these.
3. Very large
4. Marco Polo traveled along these roads.
5. The Mongols once ruled an enormous _____.
6. Discussed with

CHAPTER PREVIEW

In this chapter, you'll:

Content
► read an article by the Wright Brothers, the inventors of the airplane
► learn about many "firsts" in the history of flight

Reading Skills
► preview a passage by reading the introduction
► learn to read for the gist of a passage

Vocabulary Skills
► use words and expressions to talk about airplanes and flying
► use expressions to describe movement

Writing Skills
► describe your experiences with travel
► describe images that you find on the Internet

Internet Skills
► use the Internet to find images

SHORT SURVEY

How many times have you traveled by airplane?

❑ 0–5

❑ 6–10

❑ 11–15

❑ 16–20

❑ other _____

Reading 1:

How did Orville and Wilbur Wright become interested in flight? Read their article to find out.

Reading 2:

What are some "firsts" in air travel? Read "Flight Firsts" to find out.

Answer the questions about your flying history. Then ask your partner about his or her history. Discuss your answers.

Your Flying History

▶ Have you ever flown in an airplane? _____

   If no, explain why not. _____

▶ If you have flown, answer these questions:

1. How old were you the first time you flew in an airplane? _____

2. How many times a year do you fly? _____

3. What is the farthest distance that you have flown? _____

4. On a plane, which seat do you prefer?

   _____ aisle   _____ center   _____ window

5. If money were not important and you had to travel 500 miles, how would you travel?

   _____ plane   _____ train   _____ car   _____ other

6. How nervous are you about flying?

   _____ I'm not nervous.   _____ I'm a little nervous.

   _____ I'm very nervous.   _____ I'm frightened.

7. The best thing about flying is _____

   _____.

8. The worst thing about flying is _____

   _____.

9. Would you like to fly a plane? Why or why not? _____

   _____.

Reading 1: "On Flight" by Orville and Wilbur Wright

Before You Read

Preview

A. Reading 1, "On Flight," is by the Wright brothers, who created the first airplane. In it they describe a toy that their father gave them when they were young. What kind of toy do you think it was? Discuss your ideas with a partner.

B. The Wright brothers designed a flying machine to carry a person. Look at the picture of their plane. Discuss with your partner how planes have changed the way people live.

Vocabulary

Here are some words and expressions from "On Flight." Match each word or expression with its correct meaning. Write the letter of the meaning on the line.

Words and Expressions

_____ **1.** bat

_____ **2.** concealed

_____ **3.** dimensions

_____ **4.** excerpt

_____ **5.** furnish

_____ **6.** linear

_____ **7.** on board

_____ **8.** personal

_____ **9.** resume

_____ **10.** trial

_____ **11.** wrecked

Meanings

a. a part; not the whole

b. private

c. hidden

d. a mammal with wings

e. in a straight line

f. size (height, width, length)

g. broken

h. start again

i. provide

j. attempt; try

k. on an airplane

> I got more thrill out of flying before I had even been in the air at all—while lying in bed thinking about how exciting it would be to fly. ❧
>
> —*Orville Wright*
> *(American inventor, 1871–1948)*

As you read, think about this question:

▶ What did the Wright brothers learn from their experiments in building airplanes?

Hold fast to dreams, for if dreams die, life is a broken-winged bird that cannot fly. ❧

—*Langston Hughes*
(American poet, 1902–1967)

"On Flight," by Orville and Wilbur Wright

The following is an excerpt from an article that Orville and Wilbur Wright wrote in 1908 for a magazine. In it, they explain their childhood excitement with flying machines and how this excitement grew into the invention of the first airplane. The words are their own.

5 (Note: This article was written in 1908. It has many old-fashioned words and expressions that we don't use much today. Use the context of these old-fashioned words to try and guess the meanings of the ones you don't know.)

Our personal interest in flight dates from our childhood days. Late in the autumn of 1878, our father came into the house one evening with some object partly concealed in his hands,
10 and before we could see what it was, he tossed it into the air. Instead of falling to the floor as we expected, it flew across the room until it struck the ceiling, where it fluttered a while and finally sank to the floor. It was a little toy, known as a "hélicoptère," but we called it a "bat." It was a light frame of cork and bamboo and covered with paper. A toy so delicate lasted only a short time in the hands of small boys but its memory is abiding.

15 Several years later, we began building these hélicoptères for ourselves. To our astonishment, we found that the larger the "bat," the less it flew. We did not know that a machine having only twice the linear dimensions of another would require eight times the power. We finally became discouraged and returned to kite flying, a sport to which we had devoted so much attention that we were regarded as experts. But as
20 we became older, we had to give up this fascinating sport as unbecoming to boys our ages.

We began our active experiments in October 1900, at Kitty Hawk, North Carolina. Our machine was designed to be flown as a kite, with a man on board in winds of from 15 to 20 miles an hour. But, upon trial, it was found that much stronger winds were required to lift it. Suitable winds were not plentiful, so we found it necessary, in order to test the new balancing
25 system, to fly the machine as a kite without a man on board, operating the levers through cords from the ground.

The first flights with the power-machine were made on the 17th of December, 1903. The first flight lasted only 12 seconds, a flight very modest compared with that of birds, but it was nevertheless the first time in the history of the world in which a machine carrying a man had raised itself by its own power into the air in free flight, had sailed forward on a level course without reduction of speed, and had finally landed without being wrecked. The second and third flights were a little longer, and the fourth lasted 59 seconds, covering a distance of 852 feet over the ground against a 20-mile wind.

(. . .)

We spent 1906 and 1907 constructing new machines. In May of this year (1908), we resumed experiments (discontinued in 1905). The recent flights were made to test the ability of our machine to meet the requirements of the United States government to furnish a flyer capable of carrying two men and sufficient fuel supplies for a flight of 125 miles, with a speed of 40 miles an hour. The operator assumed a sitting position, and a seat was added for a passenger. A larger motor was installed, and radiators and gasoline reservoirs of larger capacity replaced those previously used.

Word Count: 565

Source: *San Francisco Chronicle*, original article in *Century Magazine*

Timed Reading

Read "On Flight" again. Read at a comfortable speed. Time your reading.

Start time: _____

End time: _____

My reading time: _____

After You Read

Comprehension

A. Fill in the bubble of the sentence that best describes the main idea of "On Flight."

Ⓐ The Wright brothers became interested in flight as children and, as a result, spent many years designing hélocoptères.

Ⓑ The Wright brothers became interested in flight as children, but did not remain interested as they grew older.

Ⓒ The Wright brothers became interested in flight as children and, as a result, spent many years designing airplanes.

B. Fill in the bubble for each correct answer.

1. What was the object that the Wright brothers' father brought them?

Ⓐ a kite　　　　Ⓑ a bat　　　　Ⓒ a toy flying machine

2. The Wright brothers found that the larger the "bat" was, _____.

Ⓐ the farther it flew　　　Ⓑ the faster it flew　　　Ⓒ the less it flew

3. The Wright brothers found that a machine twice as large needed _____.

Ⓐ four times the power　　Ⓑ eight times the power　　Ⓒ two times the power

4. The Wright brothers stopped flying kites because _____.

Ⓐ they quickly became experts at it　　Ⓑ they were too old to play with kites

Ⓒ they got discouraged about it

5. According to the article, the first flight in October 1900 _____.

Ⓐ did not have a man on board　　　Ⓑ had a man on board

Ⓒ had passengers on board

Reading 2: Flight Firsts

Before You Read

Preview

A. The title of Reading 2 is "Flight Firsts." What do you think the title means? What might this reading be about? Discuss your ideas with a partner.

B. Preview these words and expressions from the reading. Match each one with its correct meaning. Write the letter of the meaning on the line.

Words and Expressions	Meanings
_____ 1. adventurers	**a.** cause to move
_____ 2. aviation	**b.** the main body of an airplane
_____ 3. break the sound barrier	**c.** explorers
_____ 4. cockpit	**d.** the part of a plane where the pilot sits
_____ 5. fuselage	**e.** go faster than the speed of sound
_____ 6. propel	**f.** having to do with airplanes and flying

C. Here are some more words from "Flight Firsts." They have to do with the physical forces of flying. Match each word or expression with its correct meaning.

A Jet Airplane

Words and Expressions	Meanings
_____ 1. aerodynamic forces	**a.** movement
_____ 2. locomotion	**b.** the movement of gases, such as air
_____ 3. lift	**c.** a force that pushes something (such as air) backward so an object can move forward
_____ 4. drag	**d.** a force that pushes air downward and makes an object go upward
_____ 5. thrust	**e.** a force that opposes (acts against) the motion of an object

Using the Introduction to Preview

The introduction in a reading passage often tells you what the reading is about. You can frequently find the main ideas of a reading passage in the introduction. The introduction is usually the first paragraph or paragraphs of a passage.

Authors try to make the introduction interesting. To do this, they relate the topic of the reading to you, talk about the history of the topic, or relate it to present times. Their goal is to make you want to read more. Often the last line of the introduction tells you what to expect in the reading—what the main idea is.

For example, turn back to page 59 and read the introduction to "Cross-Cultural Exchange: 1000–1500 A.D." The introduction is the first paragraph. Notice the following:

▶ The first sentence reminds you of how the world is today.

▶ The second sentence gives an example of the information in the first sentence.

▶ The last sentence tells you what to expect in the reading passage—you will learn about extensive long-distance travel, cross-cultural exchange, and international trading.

Practice

Preview the introduction to "Flight Firsts" on page 81. The introduction is the first two paragraphs. Work with a partner to answer the following questions.

1. What does the first sentence of the introduction tell you? _____

_____

2. What do sentences two, three, four, and five of the first paragraph tell you? _____

_____

_____

_____

3. What does the last sentence of the second paragraph tell you? _____

_____

4. What do you think the reading will be about? _____

_____

As You Read

As you read, think about this question:

▶ What were some of the "firsts" in the history of flight?

🎧 Flight Firsts

Almost all ancient cultures have myths about flying. Drawings of the gods of ancient Egypt, Minoa, and Mesopotamia show them with wings. In China around 2200 B.C., people said that the emperor Shun flew over his land with the help of two large reed hats. In African stories, the great warrior Kibaga flew over his enemies and dropped rocks on
5   them. Magic carpets and flying beings appear in many myths and fairytales.

From ancient times, people have dreamed of flying, and over three hundred years ago they began to build machines to carry them through the air. In the history of flight, there have been a number of important "firsts": the first person to fly in a balloon, the first person to understand aerodynamic forces, the first person to fly in an airplane, and
10   the first person to break the sound barrier. Let's look at these and other important firsts in the history of human beings and flight.

The story of flight firsts began over three hundred years ago. The first human-operated flight occurred on November 21, 1783, when the French Montgolfier brothers flew in a hot air balloon. The brothers filled the balloon with smoke from a fire of straw, wool, and old
15   shoes. At first they didn't understand the physics of their success. They thought that the smoke caused the balloon to rise. Later, they understood that it was the hot air and not the smoke that was important. In 1784, Madame Thible, also French, became the first woman to fly in a balloon.

Hot Air Balloons

Sir George Cayley, an English scientist and inventor who
20   lived from 1773 to 1857, is sometimes called "The Father of Aviation." He earned this title because he was the first person to comprehend the four important aerodynamic forces: lift, drag, thrust, and the way the three act together. Birds use lift and thrust together by flapping their wings to fight against
25   drag. In modern airplanes, the wings don't flap. Their shape provides lift, while the engine provides thrust.

Cayley was also the first person to apply research methods to his airplane designs; he made small models first and tried to fly them before testing full-sized models. In 1799, Cayley designed the first modern airplane. It had a fixed main wing, a fuselage, a tail, a
30   cockpit for the pilot, and a way to propel the plane. His idea led to airplane propellers. The ten-year-old son of a servant was the first person to fly as the passenger in one of Cayley's inventions.

On December 17, 1903, two American brothers named Wilbur and Orville Wright flew their plane, called the "flyer," at Kitty Hawk, North Carolina. Theirs was the first powered airplane. Orville flew first, and his flight lasted 12 seconds and covered 120 feet. The winds were 27 miles an hour that day. Wilbur made four flights, with the final one lasting 59 seconds and traveling 852 feet at 10 feet in the air. In 2003, the National Aeronautics and Space Administration tried to fly a replica of the Wright brothers' plane. They researched the project for ten years and spent three years building the replica, but it would not fly and ended up in a puddle. Were the Wright brothers smart, lucky, or both?

Bessie Coleman

After the first flight, there were many more aviation firsts. Engineers invented exciting new kinds of aircraft and adventurers flew to places where planes had never gone before. For example, Louis Bleriot, both an inventor and an adventurer, designed a plane, the Bleriot XI, and in 1909 flew it from his home country of France across the English Channel to Dover, England. It was a major event, and David Lloyd George, the Chancellor of the Exchequer in Britain, was very impressed. "Flying machines are no longer toys and dreams, they are established fact," he said. "The possibilities of this new system of locomotion are infinite."

In 1910, Blanche Scott became the first woman to fly a plane alone. She also was the first woman to fly long distances (sixty miles) and the first woman test pilot. In 1922, Bessie Coleman became the first African American to earn a pilot's license.

The first big challenge in flying was getting off the ground; the next one was breaking the "sound barrier." Many pilots died trying to fly faster than the speed of sound. In 1947, in a secret U.S. government test plane called the Bell X-1, Charles Yeager succeeded. Today, planes can fly over three times the speed of sound. In 1976, the Lockheed SR flew at 2,193 miles per hour. It is still the fastest plane in history.

Word Count: 749

Source: *Celebrating the Evolution of Flight* (American Institute of Aeronautics and Astronautics)

Charles Yeager and the Bell X-1

Timed Reading

Read "Flight Firsts" again. Read at a comfortable speed. Time your reading.

Start time: _____

End time: _____

My reading time: _____

After You Read

Main Idea

Which sentence best describes the main idea of "Flight Firsts"? Fill in the bubble of the best answer.

(A) From ancient times to the present, people have dreamed of flying.

(B) Over the last 300 years, many inventors and adventurers contributed to advances in aviation.

(C) Sir George Cayley, the Wright brothers, and Madame Thible are very important in the history of flight.

Getting the Details

Answer the following questions about "Flight Firsts." Fill in the bubble for each correct answer.

1. Which statement about the Montgolfier brothers is correct?

   (A) They always thought that smoke caused their balloon to rise.

   (B) They always knew that hot air caused their balloon to rise.

   (C) They first thought that smoke caused their balloon to rise, but then they realized that hot air caused it to rise.

2. Which statement about Sir George Cayley is NOT correct?

   (A) He knew about aerodynamic forces.

   (B) He understood the way aerodynamic forces work together.

   (C) He invented aerodynamic forces.

3. Charles Yeager was the first _____.

   (A) person to fly a copy of the Wright brothers' plane

   (B) person to break the sound barrier

   (C) woman to test the Bell X-1

4. Bessie Coleman was the first _____.

  Ⓐ woman to fly alone

  Ⓑ person to break the sound barrier

  Ⓒ African American with a pilot's license

5. The Lockheed SR flew _____.

  Ⓐ the speed of sound

  Ⓑ 2,193 miles per hour

  Ⓒ over three times the speed of light

Reading Skills

Getting the Gist

Sometimes when you're reading, you don't understand every word. However, you can often get a general idea of the meaning of what you are reading without understanding every word. This is called "getting the gist" (pronounced *jist*). It is important to understand that you can be a successful reader in English even if you don't understand every word. If you understand the basic idea of what you are reading, you've gotten the gist. This can be enough.

For example, here are some sentences from "On Flight" on page 76:

> It was a little toy, known as a "hélicoptère," but we called it a "bat." It was a light frame of cork and bamboo and covered with paper. A toy so delicate lasted only a short time in the hands of small boys but its memory is abiding.

You may not know the words *cork, bamboo,* and *abiding,* but you can still get the gist of these sentences. For example, was the toy strong or weak? If you understand *lasted only a short time,* then you know that the toy was weak. Is the memory of the toy gone or still here? You know that the writers are writing about the toy now, so the memory is still here. It's a strong memory.

Practice

Below are sentences with some words that you might not know. Write the gist of each passage on the line.

1. "In China around 2200 B.C., people said that the emperor Shum flew over his land with the help of two large reed hats." You don't need to know the word *reed* to get the gist. What is the gist?

   _____

   _____

2. "The first manned flight occurred on November 21, 1783, when the French Montgolfier brothers flew in a hot air balloon." You do not need to understand the word *manned* to get the gist. What is the gist?

   _____

   _____

3. "They filled the balloon with smoke from a fire of straw, wool, and old shoes. At first they didn't understand the physics of their success. They thought that the smoke caused the balloon to rise. Later, they understood that it was the hot air and not the smoke that mattered." You don't need to understand the words *straw* or *wool* to get the gist. What is the gist?

   _____

   _____

4. "In 1799, Cayley designed the first modern airplane. It had a fixed main wing, a fuselage for gas, a tail, a cockpit for the pilot, and a way to propel the plane. His idea led to airplane propellers." You don't need to know the word *fixed* to get the gist. What is the gist?

   _____

   _____

Vocabulary

A. Here are some more words and expressions from "Flight Firsts." Find them in the reading and circle them.

Nouns	Verbs	Adjectives
gliders	fight against	fixed
replica	provides	infinite

B. Now use them to complete the sentences.

1. The possibilities for future flight are _____. There is no limit.

2. The flight took longer than usual because the plane had to _____

_____ the heavy winds that pushed it.

3. In 2003, NASA built a _____ of the Wright brothers' plane. Although it was an accurate copy, it didn't fly.

4. A burner, a stove that burns propane gas, _____ hot air for modern balloons.

5. Planes without engines are called _____.

6. The wings on Cayley's plane were _____. They didn't move.

Talk About It

Discuss these questions in small groups.

1. Would you like to ride in a hot air balloon? Why or why not?

2. Would you like to fly faster than the speed of sound? Why or why not?

3. What do you predict airplanes will be like in the future?

Would you like to ride in a hot air balloon?

I'd . . .

Expressions

Movement Expressions

Reading 1 and Reading 2 use several movement expressions that talk about movement over times, places, distances, and speeds.

Examples:
flew across (a place): We flew across Canada.
flew over (a place): Buildings look very small when you fly over them.
fly over (a speed): The Concorde could fly over three times the speed of sound.
sailed forward: The plane sailed forward for 59 seconds.
covered a distance of (a distance): The flight covered a distance of 5,000 miles.

Practice

A. Find and underline the expressions in the box above in "On Flight" or "Flight Firsts."

B. Now use them to complete the sentences. (Note: There might be more than one correct expression for some sentences.)

1. When Tina and Tim went from Los Angeles to Tokyo, they _____

   _____ the Pacific Ocean.

2. When pilots _____ _____ a mountain, they must be sure they are flying high enough.

3. The Wright brothers' plane left the ground, _____ _____, and landed safely.

4. The Wright brothers' fourth flight _____ _____

   _____ _____ 852 feet, more than seven times the distance of their first flight.

5. Charles Yeager _____ _____ the speed of sound.

Internet Research

Finding Images on the Internet

Images (pictures, photos, and diagrams) help you understand ideas. You can find images easily on the Internet. To find an image on the Internet, go to a search engine site, such as Google (www.google.com), and click on "Images." Then, type into the textbox keywords that describe the image you want to see.

Example:

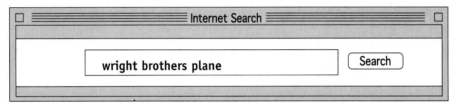

Note: You don't have to use capital letters or punctuation in a search.

Sometimes, you can also find particular images on websites that focus on certain subjects. For example, you might find pictures of early flying machines at an aviation history website, or at a website for an aviation museum, such as the Air and Space Museum at the Smithsonian Institution (www.nasm.si.edu/).

Practice

Practice looking for images on the Internet. Try to find an image of a flying machine that interests you, or one of the subjects below in the Keywords box. Use Google or an image collection at an aviation website. Print the best images and bring them to class.

Keywords		
18th century hot air balloons	Sir George Cayley	Charles Yeager and the Bell X-1
19th century hot air balloons	Blanche Scott	history of flight
hot air balloons	Bessie Coleman	how to make paper airplanes
Bleriot	cockpit	locomotion

Tell the class about your search experience. Talk about the images that you found. Explain how you found them. For example, what keywords did you use?

Write About It

A. Write the following paragraphs. Fill in the blanks. Write complete sentences.

Paragraph One

I _____ like to fly. I remember flying one time when I was
(Write *do* or *do not*)

_____. I flew from _____
(Give your age at the time)   (Give the place you started from)

to _____. I had a(n) _____
(Give your destination)   (Write *aisle*, *window*, or *center*)

seat. The flight was _____
(Use an adjective(s) to describe the ride)

because _____.
(Give a reason that supports your description)

Paragraph Two

I did an Internet search for images of aviation history. One picture that I found was of (a/an)

_____. The picture shows _____
(Say what the picture is of)

_____.
(List at least two things that you see in the picture)

The _____ is _____
(Give one thing in the picture)   (Use adjectives to describe it)

_____.

The _____ is _____.
(Give another thing in the picture)   (Use adjectives to describe it)

I _____ the picture because _____
(Write *like* or *do not like*)

_____.
(Explain what you like or do not like about the picture)

B. Now write your own paragraphs. Write one about a plane trip that you took, and another about a picture that you found on the Internet. Try to include words and expressions from this chapter in your paragraphs.

C. Write more paragraphs about your childhood, your travels, or images of flyers and flying that you found on the Internet. Use five words and expressions from the chapter and your Internet research. Choose from the following topics.

▶ Describe a childhood toy.

▶ Discuss a trip that you enjoyed and explain why you enjoyed it.

▶ Discuss a trip that you didn't enjoy and explain why you didn't enjoy it.

▶ Describe a trip that you would like to take.

▶ Explain something that you would like to invent.

▶ Describe a way airplane travel could be improved.

▶ Use your own idea.

On Your Own

Project

Give a presentation. Work in small groups. Present your ideas for improvements in air travel.

Step 1: Practice

Think about current problems with air travel and imagine ways to make improvements. Collect information on new research and developments in air travel, or use your imagination. Think about the following information:

▶ Cost of a ticket　　　　　　　　　　▶ Speed

▶ Passenger health (seats, legroom, air quality, food)　　▶ Routes

▶ Entertainment

Find or draw pictures of your suggested improvements. Write notes for your presentation. Use the box below. Practice your presentation with your group. Have your teacher listen to make sure that you are pronouncing words correctly.

Improvements in Air Travel

Step 2: Give a Presentation

Give your presentation to the class as a group. Take turns speaking. Show your pictures. Make eye contact with (look into the eyes of) your audience. The audience should take notes and ask questions afterwards.

Step 3: Follow-Up

Discuss your presentations. Which ones were interesting? What made them interesting? What will you do differently the next time you give a presentation?

Wrap Up

How Much Do You Remember?

Check your new knowledge. In this chapter you learned facts, words, and expressions. You also learned reading skills and you practiced writing. Complete the following to check what you remember.

1. What present did their father give the Wright brothers? _____

   _____

2. How long was the first airplane flight? _____

3. Who is considered the "father of aviation"? _____

4. What can you learn from the introduction to a reading? _____

   _____

5. Use *fly above* in a sentence. _____

   _____

6. When should you try to "get the gist"? _____

   _____

7. How can you find images on the Internet? _____

   _____

Second Timed Readings

Now reread "On Flight" and "Flight Firsts." Time each reading separately. Write your times in the Timed Reading Chart on page 235.

Crossword Puzzle

Complete the crossword puzzle to practice some words and expressions from this chapter.

CLUES

Across →
1. Broken
4. Size (height, length, width)
6. In a straight line
9. Cause to move
10. An attempt

Down ↓
2. Hidden
3. Movement
5. Never ending
7. Another word for a *copy*
8. Begin again

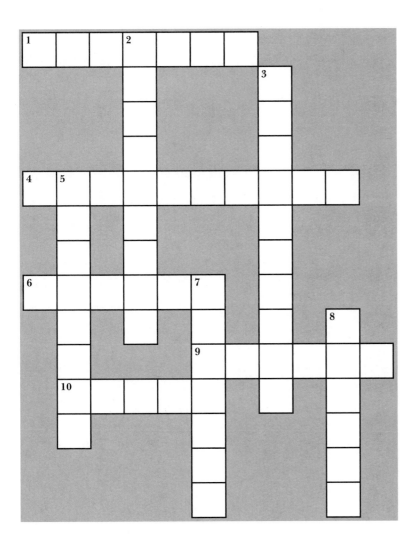

What is Business?

Business includes accounting, finance, management, marketing, and technology. Many inventors were business people who sold their inventions. Some successful business people have become very wealthy. Other areas of business include:

- corporate finance
- electronic commerce systems
- small business management
- international business

The earliest businesses were trading cattle and food crops in 9000 B.C.; the Chinese invented paper money around 900 A.D. In the 19th century, the Industrial Revolution greatly changed the world of business. By 1900, the first Masters in Business Administration program began at New York University.

SOME FAMOUS BUSINESS PEOPLE

Akio Morita—Japanese, founder of Sony, 1921–1999

Ingvar Kamprad—Swedish, founder of Ikea, 1926–

Carlos Slim Helu—Mexican, owner of Telmex, 1940–

Azim Premji—Indian, Chairman and Managing Director of Wipro, 1945–

Oprah Winfrey—American, entertainment executive, 1954–

William H. Gates III—American, founder of Microsoft, 1955–

Margaret "Meg" Whitman—American, President and CEO of eBay, 1957–

Business and You

The study of business is helpful not only in business, but also in art, engineering, medicine, biotechnology, travel, and hospitality.

Do you want to study business? Ask yourself these questions:

- Am I interested in studying a practical subject?
- Do I like to make decisions and take action?
- Can I handle stress well?
- Do I like to analyze situations?
- Am I interested in money?
- Am I interested in an international career?
- Am I good at communicating with people?

5 Jobs

CHAPTER PREVIEW

In this chapter, you'll:

Content
▶ learn how personality and jobs are connected
▶ discover what employers want from employees

Reading Skills
▶ preview a passage by reading the conclusion
▶ learn about paraphrasing

Vocabulary Skills
▶ use words and expressions to talk about personality and jobs
▶ use words and expressions to talk about job skills

Writing Skills
▶ write about your personality, your skills, and your ideal job

Internet Skills
▶ find job openings on the Internet

SHORT SURVEY

In choosing a job, the most important thing to me is:
❑ the money
❑ what time I go to work
❑ my co-workers
❑ the amount of stress in the job
❑ working in a nice place
❑ other _____

Reading 1:
How can you find a job that you will enjoy? Take a personality quiz to find out.

Reading 2:
What job skills are U.S. employers looking for? Find out in "What U.S. Employers Want."

What do you think?

Answer the questions in the box. Ask your partner the questions. Write your partner's answers in the box. Discuss your answers.

Jobs and Your Personality

	My Answers	My Partner's Answers
1. How many jobs have you had?		
2. Describe one of your jobs. What did you like about it? What didn't you like about it?*		
3. Describe your personality. What kind of person are you? (*Hint:* One definition of *personality* says that it is what makes you different from everyone else, or "unique." What makes you unique?)		
4. Psychologists say that personality doesn't change over time. Do you agree or disagree?		
5. Do you think that some personalities are good for certain jobs and not good for others? For example, if someone has the kind of personality that makes him or her a good teacher, can he or she also be a good doctor, gardener, waiter, store clerk, pilot, or artist?		

*If you have never had a job, describe the job of a friend or family member. What does that person like and dislike about the job?

Reading 1: Personality and Job Choice

Before You Read

Preview

A. The title of Reading 1 is "Personality and Job Choice." What do you think you will learn in this reading? Discuss your ideas with a partner.

B. Here are some words that describe personality types that relate to jobs. Discuss with a partner people who have these characteristics. How do they behave? Do you know someone like this? Would you like to work with someone like this?

Characteristic	Example of Behavior	Who Do You Know Like This?	Would You Like to Work with Someone Like This?
Outgoing	Likes to meet new people	My brother	Yes
Friendly			
Relaxed			
Energetic			
Careful			
Helpful			
Generous			
Nervous			
Talkative			
Patient			

Vocabulary

A. Here are some words and expressions from "Personality and Job Choice." Match each one with its correct definition below. Write the letter of the word or expression on the line.

> a. accept
> b. assigns
> c. an extrovert
> d. an introvert
> e. a leader
> f. messes up
> g. patiently
> h. rearrange
> i. refuse
> j. swings

Definitions

_____ **1.** done in a tolerant way, without complaining

_____ **2.** put in a new order

_____ **3.** makes things disorganized or not neat

_____ **4.** say "no"

_____ **5.** shy; likes to be alone

_____ **6.** gives a job or task

_____ **7.** moves back and forth

_____ **8.** say "yes"; agree

_____ **9.** someone who gives directions; the head of a group

_____ **10.** likes to be with other people

B. Use the words and expressions on pages 98 and 99 to discuss the people in the photos with a partner. What can you tell about their personalities?

As You Read

As you read, think about this question:
▶ How do personality and job choice relate to each other?

 Personality and Job Choice

When you think about getting a job, there is one very important question: What job is best for you? You might be good at something, but it may not be what you want to do for a living. For example, you may be a good gardener, but you don't like to work outside. Or you may be good at math and might be a good accountant, but you don't want to
5   work in an office all day. You want to enjoy your job, so it's important to think about what you really like to do.

Psychologists say that matching personality and type of job is very important for job happiness. To find out about your personality, take the following quiz. Your answers may give information that will help you find the job that's best for you.

10 For each question, fill in the bubble of the best answer for you.

Question 1
You go into a full classroom. Everyone looks at you. What do you do?
- (A) put your head down and quickly go to an empty seat
- (B) smile and walk slowly to a seat

15 ### Question 2
The teacher puts the students into groups. She assigns you to be the leader of your group. What do you do?
- (A) refuse and look around for someone else to do it
- (B) accept and immediately get the group started on the assignment

20 ### Question 3
Your friend asks for help with a computer problem. What do you do?
- (A) sit down and solve the problem for your friend in six minutes
- (B) tell your friend what to do and wait patiently so your friend can learn how to do it

Question 4
25 A friend asks you to help her move. What do you do?
- (A) tell her that you are busy and can't help
- (B) say, "I'll put on some old clothes. Just tell me what to do."

Question 5

Your friend has the table set up for his party. You come in and take off your coat. It swings over the table and messes up the arrangement. What do you do?

(A) carefully try and put everything back the way it was

(B) apologize many times and watch as your friend rearranges the table

Answers

Let's look at the answers and see what they mean. If you chose:

1a. You are an introvert. Look for a job where you don't have to talk to many people.

1b. You are an extrovert. Look for jobs where you work with people.

2a. You work well with a team. Look for jobs where you work in groups.

2b. You are a leader. Look for jobs where you can tell others what to do.

3a. You like to get things done. Look for a job where you can see what you finish.

3b. You like to help others. Look for a job helping people or animals.

4a. You don't like physical work. Look for a job where you work sitting down.

4b. You like physical work. Look for a job where you use your muscles.

5a. You like to solve problems. Look for a problem-solving job.

5b. You do not like to solve problems. Look for a job where you lead and others solve problems.

Word Count: 523

Source: *The Complete Idiot's Guide to Cool Jobs for Teens* (Ireland)

Timed Reading

Read "Personality and Job Choice" again. Read at a comfortable speed. Time your reading.

Start time: _____

End time: _____

My reading time: _____

After You Read

Comprehension

A. How do personality and job choice relate to each other? Fill in the bubble of the correct answer.

(A) Psychologists say that matching job and personality is important for happiness.

(B) Personality tests can help you understand which job is best for you.

(C) Both A and B

B. Fill in the bubble for each correct answer.

1. A person who likes to be around other people is probably a(n) _____.

(A) introvert   (B) extrovert   (C) leader

2. You refuse to help your friend move. According to the reading, a bad job for you is one where you _____.

(A) do physical work   (B) work sitting down   (C) work on solving problems

3. If you like to tell others what to do, you are probably a(n) _____.

(A) introvert   (B) extrovert   (C) leader

4. A person who likes to work on a team will try to _____.

(A) lead most of the time   (B) follow most of the time

(C) find out what the group needs

5. You don't like to solve problems. According to the reading, a good job for you is one where you _____.

(A) lead and have others solve problems   (B) solve problems and learn patience

(C) work outside by yourself

Talk About It

First, make a list of ten jobs. Number the jobs from 1–10. Number 1 is the job that you want most. Number 10 is the job that you want least. Then share your list with a partner and discuss why your personality does or does not match each job.

Reading 2: What U.S. Employers Want

Before You Read

Reading Skills

Previewing by Looking at the Conclusion

In Chapter 4, you learned to preview a passage by looking at the introduction. The introduction and the conclusion together are like bookends—they hold the main ideas of the passage together. You already know what kinds of information the introduction contains. The conclusion is similar: it restates the main ideas of the passage. However, it's often more specific than the introduction, and it usually reviews the most important information in the passage.

Reread the conclusion from "Cross-Cultural Exchange: 1000–1500 A.D." in Chapter 3, page 61:

> The great amount of cross-cultural exchange that happened during this time brought about important changes in the lives of the people of the eastern hemisphere. This exchange improved economies, increased the varieties of food people ate, influenced the songs they sang and the art they created, and changed the nature of warfare forever.

This conclusion talks about important changes in economies, the varieties of food people ate, the songs they sang, and the art they created. It reviews the main points of the passage. When you combine it with the information from the introduction, you get a clear idea of the main points of the passage before you read it.

Practice

Read these conclusions from various articles about jobs and try to guess the main ideas of the passages in which they appear.

1. In conclusion, you will find that there are four areas in which you can find a good job in today's economy: the professions (law, education or medicine); service, (hotels and foodservice); health-care (nursing); and business (office support, management, or sales).

   How many topics does the passage probably discuss? _____

   What are they? _____

   _____

   What do you think the main idea of this passage is? _____

   _____

2. We have looked at some of the steps in preparing for a job interview. If you do extensive reading about and are familiar with a company, think of questions to ask during the interview, consult with people who work there, dress in clean, appropriate clothes, and come to the interview well rested and on time, you will have a good chance of getting the job.

How many topics does the passage probably discuss? _____

What are they? _____

_____

What do you think the main idea of this passage is? _____

_____

3. There are many good sources to help you find a job. Remind your friends that you are looking for a job, go on the Internet, read the newspaper, call the company you'd like to work for, and meet with a job counselor.

How many topics does the passage probably discuss? _____

What are they? _____

_____

What do you think the main idea of this passage is? _____

_____

4. Bob Mathews said that he is looking for young, hard-working employees who are good readers and writers and who are willing to learn. He is your average employer. Most employers are looking for the same things.

How many topics does the passage probably discuss? _____

What are they? _____

_____

What do you think the main idea of this passage is? _____

_____

Preview

A. Read the introduction and the conclusion to "What U.S. Employers Want" on pages 106 and 107. How many skills do U.S. employers want? What are they? What do you think the main idea of this passage is? Discuss these questions with a partner.

B. Preview these words from the reading. Complete each of the sentences below with the correct word.

appropriately	commission	logic	participate in
percentages	revise	self-image	trust

1. John's boss likes him a lot because John is very honest. The boss feels he can

_____ John.

2. Kevin is good at math. For example, he can easily find 50% of 250 or 25% of 90. He can do

_____ very well.

3. Sara will probably be a good employee because she likes herself. She has a positive

_____ .

4. The government wanted to find out what employers are looking for, so they organized a

group of people to do research. This _____ found three main things

that employers want.

5. Alex has a very organized mind. For example, he can easily see causes and effects.

This is because he uses _____ .

6. Ray always dresses well for a job interview. He wears a clean shirt, a tie, and a nice suit. He

dresses _____ for every interview.

7. Janet speaks well and has a lot of great ideas. She likes to _____

_____ group discussions, and people like to hear her ideas.

8. Tara's boss read her report and asked her to make some changes. Tara liked the ideas her

boss suggested and was happy to _____ the report.

As you read, think about this question:

▶ What do U.S. employers want from their employees?

> An individual's self-concept is the core of . . . personality. It affects every aspect of human behavior: the ability to learn, the capacity to grow and change . . . A strong, positive self-image is the best possible preparation for success in life. ❧
>
> —*Joyce Brothers (American psychologist and author, b. 1928)*

What U.S. Employers Want

To get a great job, you need to show employers that you have what they are looking for. In the early 1990s, the United States Secretary of Commerce created a commission to look at what employers want from employees. This, along with other research, shows that all employers want the same things from employees. They want basic skills, thinking skills, and person-
5 al qualities, such as honesty and self-esteem. Employers want these skills and qualities in all employees regardless of profession—from accountants to baseball players, computer workers to salespeople, and chefs to teachers. Think about your strengths in these three areas when you look for a job. Be ready to talk about your strengths during a job interview. You want to be specific, so let's look closely at what employers want.

Basic Skills

10 Employers want people who know the basic skills of reading, writing, and arithmetic. They also want employees who listen and speak well.

To employers, reading means understanding written information. This information may be in sentences, paragraphs, charts, graphs, or schedules. Employees must be able to write messages, letters, directions, and reports. Sometimes, they must also be prepared to make
15 graphs and charts. For arithmetic, employers are looking for people who can add, subtract, multiply, and divide. Employees must know how to do percentages. They must be able to give estimates without a calculator.

Employers also want employees who can listen and respond to what someone says. In speaking, employers are looking for people who give information in an organized way. They
20 want employees to participate in discussions, and they especially like people who ask questions and can understand and use body language. Researchers say that 80 percent of the information in any face-to-face communication comes from body language, such as eye contact, posture, and facial expression. Employees must use body language to show speakers that
25 they are listening and that they understand the speaker.

Thinking Skills

There are six types of thinking skills that are important to employers: creative thinking, decision-making, problem-solving, seeing things in your mind's eye, knowing how to learn, and reasoning.

Creative thinking means coming up with new ideas. Decision-making means thinking about risks, evaluating alternatives, and choosing the best alternative. The first step in problem-solving is recognizing that there is a problem. Then an employee has to find the reasons for the problem and think of a plan to solve it. In problem-solving, the employee must also be willing to revise the solution if necessary. Employees who can see things in their mind's eye are able to picture a diagram and imagine the real object that it represents. They can also imagine going through several steps in completing a job, even when reading about it or listening to someone explain it. Knowing how to learn means knowing how to find and learn new information. Reasoning means seeing the relationship between things; it means using logic to form conclusions. In addition, it means using old knowledge in new situations.

Personal Qualities

There are five personal qualities employers are looking for: responsibility, self-esteem, sociability, self-management, and honesty.

To employers, responsibility means that an employee works hard to do an excellent job. The employee pays attention to details. The employee also does unpleasant tasks well. Of course, the employee comes on time and lets the employer know if there is a problem. Employers want people with self-esteem, people who like themselves. They want employees with a positive self-image. Employees who are insecure make others uncomfortable. Friendliness and politeness are two aspects of sociability. Everyone likes to be around friendly and polite people. Employers don't want to tell employees what to do all the time, so they are looking for people with self-management skills. These people can set their own goals and meet those goals. People with good self-management skills don't show anger when someone criticizes them. Honesty is also important. Everyone likes to be around people they trust.

Basic skills, thinking skills, and personality skills are the abilities needed in the 21st century workplace. Think of examples that you can use during a job interview to show that you have these skills.

Word Count: 686

Source: "What U.S. Employers Want—The Secretary's Commission on Achieving Necessary Skills (SCANS)" (U.S. Department of Labor).

Timed Reading

Read "What U.S. Employers Want" again.
Read at a comfortable speed. Time your reading.

Start time: _____

End time: _____

My reading time: _____

After You Read

Main Idea

Which sentence best describes the main idea of "What U.S. Employers Want"? Fill in the bubble of the best answer.

(A) U.S. employers want employees who know how to use a calculator and leave clear phone messages.

(B) U.S. employers want employees who have basic skills, thinking skills, and personal qualities.

(C) U.S. employers usually want responsible, polite employees who are honest and friendly.

Reading Skills

Paraphrasing

Paraphrasing is putting other people's ideas into your own words. It's a great reading skill because if you can correctly paraphrase an author's ideas, it means that you really understand them. When you paraphrase an author's ideas either orally or in writing, it can also help you remember important information. Here's an example from "Personality and Job Choice" on page 100:

Original words: When you think about getting a job, there is one most important question: What job is best for you? You might be good at something, but it may not be what you want to do for a living. For example, you may be a good gardener, but you don't like to work outside. Or you may be good at math and might be a good accountant, but you don't want to work in an office all day. You want to enjoy your job, so it's important to think about what you really like to do.

Paraphrase: To find the job that's right for you, thinking about what you like is more important than thinking about what you're good at.

Notice that the paraphrase uses synonyms (for example, *think about getting* becomes *to find; what you really like to do* becomes *what you like*) and different sentence structure.

Practice

A. Practice paraphrasing ideas from "What U.S. Employers Want." Read the original words and write a paraphrase on the lines.

1. **Original:** In speaking, employers are looking for employees who give information in an organized way. They want employees to participate in discussions, and they especially like employees who ask questions and can understand and use body language.

   Paraphrase: _____

   _____

2. **Original:** The first step in problem-solving is recognizing that there is a problem. Then an employee has to find the reasons for the problem and think of a plan to solve it. In problem-solving, the employee must also be willing revise the solution if necessary.

   Paraphrase: _____

   _____

3. **Original:** To employers, responsibility means that an employee works hard to do an excellent job. The employee pays attention to details. The employee also does unpleasant tasks well. Of course, the employee comes on time and lets the employer know if there is a problem.

   Paraphrase: _____

   _____

B. Apply your knowledge. Read the situations below. Based on "What U.S. Employers Want" answer the questions on a separate piece of paper. Then compare your answers with a partner.

1. Johanna is good at problem-solving. She has good listening and speaking skills. She is friendly and polite. She would like to be a manager at a fast-food restaurant. Will an employer want to hire her? Why or why not?

2. Rob is dressed appropriately for the interview. He is good at decision-making and is logical. However, he did not look the interviewer in the eye during the interview. Will the employer want to hire him? Why or why not?

3. James dresses well for interviews. He can read and write English well, but he does not know how to do percentages or estimates. Will most employers be happy to hire him? Why or why not?

4. Tom can speak, read, and write well in English. He is always dressed appropriately. He uses appropriate body language and knows how to learn. He wants a job as a front desk clerk at a hotel. Will an employer want to hire him? Why or why not?

5. Rachel speaks and reads well. She is a creative thinker and is friendly and responsible, but she doesn't listen well. Will most employers want to hire her? Why or why not?

Vocabulary

A. Here are some more words from "What U.S. Employers Want." Find them in the reading and circle them.

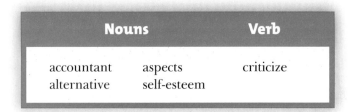

Nouns		Verb
accountant	aspects	criticize
alternative	self-esteem	

B. Now use them to complete the sentences.

1. David needs to have a more positive self-image. His _____ is low and employers usually don't like that.

2. It's important to look at all sides of a problem. If you examine all _____ of a problem, it's easier to find a solution.

3. Employers like Mark because when they tell him that he has done something wrong, he has

   a positive reaction. He accepts their comments when they _____ him.

4. Ted likes to work with numbers. He is very organized and keeps his checkbook in order. He

   will make a good_____.

5. There are two job choices for you. Which _____ do you like best?

Talk About It

Discuss these questions in small groups.

1. Which three of the five basic skills do you think are most important for each of the following positions: an accountant, a chef, a gardener? Why?

2. Which four of the six thinking skills do you think are most important for each of the following positions: a professional baseball player, a salesperson, a first-grade teacher? Why?

Expressions

> ## Expressions Describing Job Skills
>
> Some expressions used to describe job skills contain the *-ing* form of a verb.
>
> **creative thinking**   **evaluating alternatives**   **problem-solving**
> **decision-making**   **knowing how to learn**   **thinking skills**
>
> **Example:**
> They want basic skills, thinking skills, and personal qualities.
>
> **Note:** Some of these *-ing* forms are gerunds (nouns) and some are participles (adjectives).

Practice

A. Find and underline the *-ing* expressions from the box in "Personality and Job Choice" or "What U.S. Employers Want."

B. Now use some of them to complete the sentences.

1. If there is a problem, Josh can find a solution. _____-_____ is one of his job skills.

2. Claire has a good imagination. Because of her _____ _____, she is always thinking of new ideas.

3. Steven is good at thinking about all possibilities and then deciding which choices are good and which ones are not. _____ _____ is one of his strengths.

4. Aaron's teachers and bosses like him because if he doesn't know something, he learns about it. _____ _____ _____ _____ is one of his most valuable skills.

5. Many people have a hard time deciding things. If an employer knows you are good at _____-_____ then he or she may be interested in hiring you.

Internet Research

Finding and Reading Job Descriptions on the Internet

Most big companies list job openings on their websites. Job listings are usually not on the homepage (the first page) of the website. However, you can usually find on the homepage listed links to *Careers, Jobs, Hiring Opportunities, About Us, Our Company,* or *Company Information.* For example, if you go to the home-page for *Ben and Jerry's* (an ice cream company), and click on *Our Company,* this will take you to a page with a *Jobs* link. Click on that link to find information about jobs at Ben and Jerry's.

Practice

Practice looking for jobs on the Internet. Choose three or more companies that you are interested in or from the Keywords box below. Look for information about jobs at those companies. Print out a description of the jobs that interest you. Circle any skills in the job descriptions that match the ones you have read about in this chapter.

Keywords		
Coca-Cola jobs	Mitsubishi jobs	Sheraton Hotel jobs
Ikea jobs	Round Table Pizza jobs	Starbucks jobs

Tell the class about the job descriptions you chose.

Write About It

A. Write the following paragraphs. Fill in the blanks. Write complete sentences.

Paragraph One

I have skills and personal qualities that employers want. One of my basic skills is

_____.

(List one basic skill)

For example, _____

_____.

(Give an example of this skill)

My thinking skills include _____

(List one thinking skill)

For example, _____

_____.

(Give an example of this skill)

I have good personal qualities, too. One of my personal qualities is _____

_____.

(Give an example of a personal quality)

For example, _____

_____.

(Give an example of this quality)

Paragraph Two

My ideal job is _____.

(Name your ideal job)

There are several reasons why this is my ideal job. One reason is (that) _____

_____.

(Give one reason this is your ideal job)

Another reason _____ is my ideal job is (that) _____
               (Re-state the name of the job)

_____ .
                              (Give another reason this is your ideal job)

Finally, this is also the best job for me because _____

_____ .
                              (Give another reason this is your ideal job)

B. Now write your own paragraphs. Write one paragraph about your job skills, another about your personal qualities, and a third about the best job for you. Write each paragraph two times. First, imagine that the reader is a friend of yours. Then imagine that the reader is a possible employer.

C. Write more paragraphs about personality, job skills, personal qualities, and job choice. Use five words and expressions from this chapter and your Internet research. Choose from the following topics.

▶ Write about a friend or family member who is working. Describe his or her personality and job. Are they a good match? Why or why not?

▶ Write about a specific job. What qualities does someone doing that job need? If you were the boss, what would you look for?

▶ Recommend a friend or family member for a job. Describe the person and explain why he or she is good for the job.

▶ Use your own idea.

> Few things help an individual more than to place responsibility upon him, and to let him know that you trust him. ∂▲
>
> —Booker T. Washington (African American inventor, president of Tuskegee Institute, and presidential advisor, 1856–1915)

On Your Own

Project

Design a job interview questionnaire and practice asking and answering the questions.

Step 1: Practice

Get into small groups. Think of a job and write a brief description of it. You may want to look at the results of the Internet search you did earlier. Next, write seven job interview questions for people who might want the job.

Examples:
1. Do you have good basic skills? Explain.
2. Give an example of your decision-making skills.
3. Are you an honest person? Give an example.

Step 2: Do the Interview

Meet with another group and get into pairs. Ask and answer the interview questions that your group wrote.

Step 3: Follow-Up

Evaluate your success. Which of your questions were good? Why? Which of your questions were not good? Why?

John Harrison, Edy's Ice Cream Tester

Wrap Up

How Much Do You Remember?

Check your new knowledge. In this chapter you learned facts, words, and expressions. You also learned reading skills and you practiced writing. Complete the following to check what you remember.

1. If you are an *introvert*, what kind of job is good for you? _____

    _____

2. If you are an *extrovert*, what kind of job is good for you? _____

    _____

3. What are two parts of a reading passage that you can use to preview the passage?_____

    _____

4. What are *basic skills*? _____

    _____

5. What is *self-esteem*? _____

    _____

6. Use *decision-making* in a sentence. _____

    _____

7. How can you find job opportunities on the Internet? _____

    _____

Second Timed Readings

Now reread "Personality and Job Choice" and "What U.S. Employers Want." Time each reading separately. Write your times in the Timed Reading Chart on page 236.

Crossword Puzzle

Complete the crossword puzzle to practice some words and expressions from this chapter.

CLUES

Across →

1. Changes something from neat to not neat
5. Janet likes to _____ in group discussions.
7. Change; do over
9. Agree
10. Feelings about oneself

Down ↓

2. Moves back and forth
3. Choice
4. A group of people who do research on a subject
6. Someone who guides a group
8. Say *no*

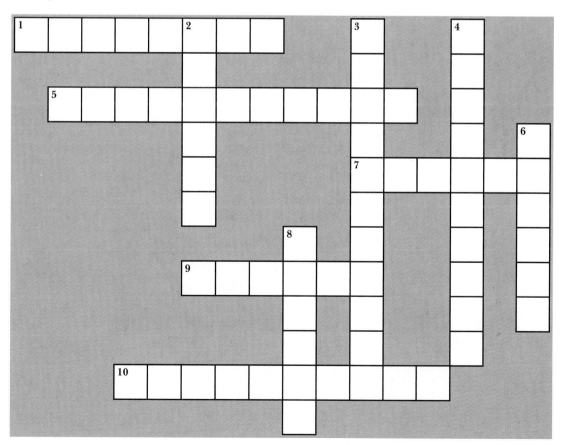

CHAPTER PREVIEW

In this chapter, you'll:

Content
▶ learn how products get their names
▶ discover what marketers think about before they sell a product internationally

Reading Skills
▶ preview a reading by putting several strategies together
▶ take notes as you read

Vocabulary Skills
▶ use words and expressions to talk about marketing
▶ use words and expressions to talk about culture
▶ use verb + infinitive combinations to discuss international marketing

Writing Skills
▶ write about successful marketing, companies, products, and advertising

Internet Skills
▶ limit search results on the Internet

> Everyone lives by selling something. 🐌
>
> —Robert Louis Stevenson (Scottish novelist, poet, and essayist, 1850–1894)

SHORT SURVEY

When I buy new clothes, the most important thing to me is:

❑ the style
❑ their popularity
❑ the brand name
❑ the fit
❑ the color
❑ other _____

Reading 1:

How do companies choose brand names? Read an interview with a branding consultant to find out.

Reading 2:

Why is a Swedish furniture company so successful in countries around the world? Find out in "International Marketing: Strategies for Success."

Answer the questions in the box. Compare your answers with a partner.

Brands and You

A *brand* is a name, a word, an idea, a design, or a picture that identifies a company's product. A brand can be one product, a group of products, or all of a company's products. For example, Dell is a brand of computers. Companies choose brand names carefully because they want you to notice and like them. They also want to make their products seem different from other companies' products. Companies hope that you remember their brands, but how important are brands to *you*?

1. **When you buy a product, how important to you is the brand name?**

   Very important   Somewhat important   Not important at all

2. **Do you ever <u>not</u> buy something because you do not like the product name?**

   Yes   No

   Give an example: _____

3. **When you buy a product, how important to you is the advertising for that product?**

   Very important   Somewhat important   Not important at all

4. **Look at the following brand names. Choose one brand and answer the questions below.**

   Apple computers   Evian mineral water   Benetton clothing
   Ikea furniture   Microsoft software   Mitsubishi automobiles
   Nike athletic shoes/clothing   Swatch watches   Other _____

- Are you familiar with this brand name? If yes, what is your opinion of the product or company?

   _____

- What does this brand name make you think of? For example, *fun, quality, youth,* etc.

   _____

- Which ads for this product or company do you like?

   _____

Reading 1: An Interview with a Branding Consultant

Before You Read

Preview

A. The title of Reading 1 is "An Interview with a Branding Consultant." What kind of information might this reading include? Discuss your ideas with a partner.

B. Give your opinion of some product names. Read this list of possible names for companies, products, or services. (It doesn't matter what companies, products, or services they are for.) First, say them out loud and think about how they sound. For example, do they sound nice, silly, sad, or unattractive? List adjectives that describe how they sound to you.

Then think about what each name suggests. That is, what does it make you think of? List idea words (nouns) that each name suggests, such as *freedom, strength,* and *happiness.*

Name	How Does It Sound? (Adjectives)	What Does It Suggest? (Nouns)
Aero		
Aviara		
Bondi		
Festiva		
Sahara		
Sportiva		
Stella		
Venturi		

Vocabulary

Here are some words and expressions from "An Interview with a Branding Consultant." Complete each of the sentences below with the correct word or expression.

analyze	associations	branding	corporations
evaluate	(be) familiar with	market	model

1. _____ is giving names to products, companies, and services.

2. Dr. Clark's job is to _____ names. She decides whether they are good or bad names for certain products.

3. A large company asked Dr. Clark to _____their new product names. They wanted someone to study them carefully before they used them in a foreign country.

4. I'm _____ _____ Japanese and Spanish. I studied both languages in college and I know them pretty well.

5. _____ can be either large or small companies. An example of a large one is Microsoft; a small one is Resolution Biosciences.

6. Many companies want to _____ to young people. They do extensive interviews with young people in order to learn how to best sell products and services to them.

7. Some cultures have negative _____ with certain colors. For example, the color black makes North Americans think of death.

8. In 2003, Volkswagen started selling a new car _____ called the "Touareg." Many people thought that this was a strange name for a car.

As You Read

As you read, think about this question:

▶ What does a branding consultant do?

🎧 An Interview with a Branding Consultant

Mike Malone interviewed Dr. Lynn Clark, a linguist (someone who studies languages). Dr. Clark helps new companies choose product names. Read their interview:

MM: Thanks for agreeing to this interview. Let's start with your background.
5 How did you become a branding consultant?

LC: Companies come to me because I have a Ph.D. in linguistics from Harvard University, and I have 20 years experience studying languages. As a linguist, I'm familiar with the sounds and sentence structure of many languages. I also study whole words, parts of words, and word meanings.

10 **MM:** But what does linguistics have to do with branding?

LC: Well, many of the companies that I work for do business internationally.

MM: Why do international corporations need you?

LC: To make money, international corporations need to fit well into the cultures of the countries where they do business. This is where language becomes
15 important. Product names have to sound "right" in a culture. They hire me to evaluate their ideas.

MM: What do you mean?

LC: Well, first of all, you can't directly translate a brand name from one language into another. For example, Fiat, the Italian car company, had a model called
20 "Uno." *Uno* means *number one* in Italian. A linguist helped them rename the model for Finland, though, because *uno* means *garbage* in Finnish.

MM: I see . . . you make sure a name or sound isn't unattractive.

LC: Exactly. Names shouldn't be silly or sad, either. Also, certain sounds have associations with them. For example, in English, the /i/ sound (as in the word *speed*) gives the idea of speed. A Japanese company asked me to help them choose a name for a running shoe to market in the U.S. I gave them several possible names with the /i/ sound in it. I can't tell you the name that they chose, but some of the possibilities that they liked were Via, Zenith, and Sleek.

MM: Don't words have other associations?

LC: Yes, they do. I also analyze associations with word meanings. *Tree*, for example, is associated with being strong and tall in English. I also check for word associations in other languages. I look at the Greek and Latin roots of words, too.

MM: Can you give an example?

LC: Yes. *Avi* is a Latin root that means *bird*. An example of an airline company that uses the root avi is Avianca.

MM: You must know a lot of languages!

LC: I know English, French, German, Italian, Japanese, Portuguese, and Spanish.

MM: That's very impressive. Thanks so much for your time.

LC: You're welcome.

Word Count: 426

Source: Personal communication

Timed Reading

Read "An Interview with a Branding Consultant" again. Read at a comfortable speed. Time your reading.

Start time: _____

End time: _____

My reading time: _____

After You Read

Comprehension

A. What does a branding consultant do for companies that want to sell products in different countries? Fill in the bubble of the correct answer.

    (A) Analyze the sounds in new product names.

    (B) Analyze the possible meanings of new product names.

    (C) Both A and B

B. Fill in the bubble for each correct answer.

1. Linguists are good people to evaluate product names because they understand _____.

    (A) how corporations work   (B) many languages   (C) the politics of many countries

2. International companies must choose product names carefully because the names must be

    (A) legally correct   (B) technically correct   (C) culturally correct

3. According to Dr. Clark, what does the sound /i/ in English suggest?

    (A) youth   (B) strength   (C) speed

4. According to Dr. Clark, which product name might be good for a package delivery company in the United States?

    (A) Zee   (B) Rock   (C) Apple

5. According to Dr. Clark, what does the Latin root *avi* mean?

    (A) tree   (B) speed   (C) bird

Talk About It

Work with a partner and make up names for the following products: a new soft drink, a new kind of athletic shoe, and a new car. Decide who you want to sell the products to (senior citizens, adults, young adults, teens, or children) and explain why you think the names you created are good. Think about both the sounds of the names and the meanings associated with the words or word parts in the names.

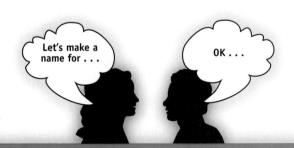

Reading 2: International Marketing: Strategies for Success

Before You Read

Reading Skills

> ### Review: Using the Strategies Together
>
> In previous chapters, you learned to prepare mentally and physically for reading, and you used personal experience to connect with a topic. You also used titles and headings to predict main ideas and details, and in Chapters 4 and 5 you previewed a passage by reading the introduction and the conclusion. Good readers use all of these strategies to prepare for reading. Here's one way to put them all together:
>
> 1. Before you start, create a positive attitude and find a comfortable place to read.
> 2. Think about the topic and connect it to your experiences. Think about what you already know about the topic.
> 3. Now read the title. Think about the main idea of the reading. Think beyond the main idea and guess details.
> 4. Read the section headings. Think about what might be in each section to preview the supporting details.
> 5. Read the introduction to find a main idea statement. Read the conclusion for a summary of the main ideas.

Practice

Practice using topic, title, headings, and the introduction and conclusion to preview a reading passage. Look at "International Marketing: Strategies for Success" on pages 127 and 128. Work with a partner and answer the questions below on a separate piece of paper.

1. The topic of the reading passage is international marketing—planning for and selling products in different countries. What questions can you ask yourself to connect to the topic?

2. Look at the title. What do you think the reading passage might be about?

3. Look at the headings for each section. What do you think each section might be about?

4. Read the introduction and the conclusion. Can you find a main idea statement? Underline it. Does it confirm your guesses so far?

5. Now make a prediction: What do you think the main idea and supporting ideas in this reading are?

Preview

A. The title of Reading 2 is "International Marketing: Strategies for Success." What kind of information might this reading include? Discuss your opinions with a partner.

B. Preview these words and expressions from the reading. Complete each of the sentences below with the correct word.

brand loyalty	consumers	entering a market	market
marketers	marketing	slogan	values

1. Another word for *selling* is _____.

2. People, companies, or organizations that sell something are called _____.

3. People who buy things are called _____.

4. Anything from a small store to an entire country can be a _____, a place where people buy and sell things.

5. Companies must think about many things before they start selling their products in a particular place because it's important to know as much as possible before

   _____ _____ _____.

6. People who buy the same products over and over again because they like them practice

   _____ _____.

7. Ad writers often create funny, memorable sayings about products because a funny

   _____ often helps customers remember the product name better.

8. _____ are ideas that a group of people has about what is important and how to behave. These ideas often vary from culture to culture.

As You Read

As you read, think about this question:
▶ What do companies have to think about before they
sell products internationally?

🎧 International Marketing: Strategies for Success

What do the Swatch watch company, the Ikea furniture company, and HSBC
banking all have in common? They are all large companies that successfully sell
products or services around the globe. This is not easy, because people in different
countries such as the United Kingdom, China, or Greece often want different
5 things. What makes people decide to buy things (consumer behavior) varies from
culture to culture. Companies that choose to do business internationally must
do a thorough analysis of the cultures where they want to sell their products or
services.

International Marketing and Culture

Culture is the language, customs, tastes, attitudes, lifestyles, and values of a
10 group of people. Marketers must understand these characteristics before they
design products, name them, or advertise them in different countries. For example, American culture emphasizes individuality and nonconformance. Japanese
culture, on the other hand, emphasizes cooperation and conformity. Therefore,
American marketers who plan to sell goods in Japan need to create advertising
15 messages that do not overemphasize individuality and nonconformance.

In addition, international marketers need to understand how to communicate
with consumers in the cultures where they want to sell products. Communicating
effectively with a particular culture involves understanding the language, as well
as the images, colors, and ideas about design that work in the culture. For exam-
20 ple, marketers need to know that they should not use the color green in Malaysia,
because it symbolizes death and disease in that culture.

The Risks of Ignoring Culture

When companies do not analyze the cultures where they plan to do business, they may experience poor sales or worse—they may insult the culture. This can damage the company's image in that country. These mistakes are very expensive. Look at these three famous international marketing mistakes:

- An American pen company advertised a new kind of pen in Mexico that did not leak in your pocket. The company directly translated into Spanish their English slogan, "It won't leak in your pocket and embarrass you." The company used the word *embarazar* for "embarrass". This was a terrible mistake. Why? Because in Spanish the actual meaning of the ad was "It won't leak in your pocket and make you pregnant." (*Embarazar* means "to make pregnant" in Spanish.

- Several years ago, a drink company sold a popular fruit drink with pulp (tiny pieces of fruit) in it. It was popular in the U.S., so they decided to sell it in Japan. No one bought it. Why? The drink sold well in the U.S. because in American culture, fruit pulp means a drink is "fresh and healthy." However, at that time, in Japanese culture fruit pulp in a drink meant "poor quality." Nowadays, the trend has changed. In Japan fruit pulp is seen as a healthy fruit juice ingredient.

- A European drug company used a visual marketing campaign to sell a headache tablet in the Middle East. It used three photos. The one on the left showed a man looking unhappy, enduring a miserable headache; the one in the middle showed the man taking a pill; the one on the right showed the man looking happy. The mistake? Arabic speakers "read" messages (including photos) from right to left, so the consumers saw the message: "If you're happy, take our pill and you will be miserable."

Getting It Right: A Case Study

Advertising is the most important way that companies can get consumers to buy their products. When companies design advertising messages to match the countries and cultures where they do business, they increase sales and create brand loyalty. An example of a company that successfully sells throughout the world is Ikea.

A Swedish furniture company, Ikea has been successful around the world, but particularly in Germany, Canada, and the United States. Ikea analyzed the fur-

niture-buying behavior of each market before entering it and used local advertising agencies to create warm, humorous ads for each country. For example,
Canadian ads gently poked fun at Sweden. Making fun of Swedes doesn't work
in American culture, so U.S. ads showed modern American "families" buying
furniture.

It's easy to see that international companies need to pay attention to the
cultures where they want to do business. Companies that take the time to plan for
international marketing will always be more successful than those that don't.

Word Count: 711

Source: *Global Marketing* (Johansson)

Timed Reading

Read "International Marketing: Strategies for
Success" again. Read at a comfortable speed.
Time your reading.

Start time: _____

End time: _____

My reading time: _____ minutes

After You Read

Main Idea

Which sentence best describes the main idea of "International Marketing: Strategies for Success"? Fill in the bubble of the best answer.

(A) Ikea, a Swedish furniture company, is successful because it knows a lot about the cultures of the places where it sells products.

(B) International marketers must know the meanings of different colors in different cultures.

(C) To be successful, international marketers must learn about the cultures and the languages of the places where they want to sell products.

Getting the Details

A. Answer the following questions about "International Marketing: Strategies for Success."

1. What is one difference between Japanese values and American values? _____

   _____

2. What's an example of why it's important to know what certain colors mean in different

   cultures? _____

   _____

3. In the past, why didn't an American drink with fruit pulp sell in Japan? _____

   _____

4. How does well-designed advertising help a company sell products overseas? _____

   _____

5. What's an example of a company that has good international advertising? _____

   _____

Reading Skills

Taking Notes as You Read

Good readers take notes as they read a passage. This helps them pay attention to and retain important information.

There are many ways to take notes as you read. Here are some ideas:
- Write in the margins (the white spaces around the passage) your questions about the reading. Underline things that you agree or disagree with, ideas that you like or can connect with, or items you want more information about. Draw lines from your notes to words in the passage to identify a connection.
- Circle, mark with a star (*), or draw a box around important dates and numbers, or words that you don't know.

Let's look at an example from Chapter 5:

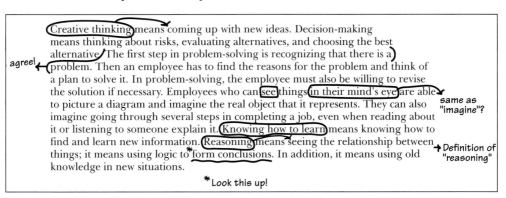

Practice

Read "International Marketing: Strategies for Success" again. As you read, write notes in the margins. Circle, box, or mark with a star numbers, dates, and unclear words. Draw lines from your notes to the numbers, dates, and words. Take notes on the following:
- ▶ information that answers the pre-reading question
- ▶ ideas that you agree or disagree with
- ▶ questions you have about the information in the passage
- ▶ what you still want to know about the topic

Compare your notes with a partner.

Vocabulary

A. Here are some more words and expressions from "International Marketing: Strategies for Success." Find them in the reading and circle them.

Nouns	Verbs	Adverbs
conformity	have in common	effectively
manufacturer	poked fun at	
retailer		

B. Now use them to complete the sentences.

1. In addition to being a _____, Svenska Furniture Company also has a chain of stores around the world.

2. What do Ikea and Svenska Furniture _____ _____ _____? They are both successful Swedish furniture companies.

3. Ikea's Canadian ads _____ _____ _____ Swedish culture. Canadians really liked them because the ads made jokes about the Swedes.

4. Marketing _____ in different countries has made Ikea popular around the world. For them, marketing their products carefully and appropriately has increased their sales.

5. Nike not only makes athletic shoes and clothing, but it has also become a _____. They now have their own shops in several major cities.

6. Being alike is important in Japanese culture. On the other hand, _____ is not valued in the United States.

Talk About It

Discuss these questions.

1. Are you familiar with Swatch watches? If yes, what is you opinion of them? Have you seen any Swatch ads? If yes, what is your opinion of them?

2. Are you familiar with Ikea furniture? If yes, what is your opinion of it? Have you seen any Ikea ads? If yes, what is your opinion of them?

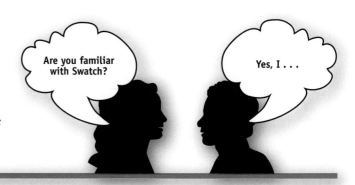

Are you familiar with Swatch?

Yes, I . . .

Expressions

> ## Verb and Infinitive Combinations for Talking about Marketing
>
> Certain verb + infinitive combinations are useful in talking about business. An infinitive is the simple form of a verb with "to" in front of it.
>
> | | | |
> |---|---|---|
> | **choose to do business** | **decide to buy** | **hope to sell** |
> | **need to fit well into** | **planned to market** | **wants to sell** |
>
> **Example:**
> This will be good for a company that wants to sell food in an English-speaking country.

Practice

A. Find and underline these verb + infinitive combinations in the box in "An Interview with a Branding Consultant" or "International Marketing."

B. Now use them to complete the sentences.

1. A company that _____ _____ _____ a soft drink in Japan probably should not emphasize individuality in their ads.

2. A company's product names _____ _____ _____

   _____ _____ a culture; otherwise, the company may lose money or worse, insult the culture.

3. Several years ago, Snapple _____ _____ _____ an American fruit drink in Japan, but after they analyzed consumer behavior, they decided not to enter the market.

4. BeautySpot products are successful in Europe; now they _____ _____

   _____ their cosmetics in Asia, as well.

5. If you _____ _____ _____ _____ in another country, you must first carefully study the country's culture.

6. Consumers _____ _____ _____ products for many reasons; the product's name, its quality, and its advertising all influence consumer behavior.

Internet Research

Limiting Search Results

When you do a search on the Internet, sometimes you get *too much* information. For example, if you search using the word *Nike,* you can get over 6,600,000 results! The term *Nike* alone is very general, and people use it in many contexts. In this case, you need to limit your search.

Here's how to limit a search: The first step is to combine keywords. This gives you more precise results. For example, let's say that you want to get information about Nike ads. If you use the keywords *Nike ads,* you'll get fewer results (about 156,000) than with the word *Nike* alone, and the results are more likely to be on the topic that you are interested in.

The second step is to use quotation marks around your keywords. This gives you results that include the keywords together as a phrase; the results will be even more precise. For example, if you put quotation marks around *"Nike ads,"* you'll only get around 2,600 results.

Practice

Practice using keyword combinations and quotations to limit a search. Find information about international companies. First, use general terms. Then combine keywords. Finally, put quotations around keyword combinations. Compare your results. Try using the following keyword combinations, or use your own.

Keywords
(company name)
(company name) news
(company name) ads
(company name) print ads
(company name) TV ads
(company name) marketing
(company name) international marketing

Tell the class about your experience.

Write About It

A. Write the following paragraphs. Fill in the blanks. Write complete sentences.

Paragraph One

International marketers need to do many things before they sell products or services overseas.

One thing that they must do is _____.
(State one thing that they must do)

They must do this because _____

_____.
(Explain why this is important)

Another thing they must do is _____.
(State another thing that they must do)

This is important because _____

_____.
(Explain why this is important)

Paragraph Two

_____ is very successful for two reasons. One
(Give a company, a product, a product name, or identify an ad)

reason it's successful is that _____
(Give one reason why this company/product/name/ad is successful)

_____.

For example, _____.
(Give a specific example that supports the reason)

Another reason it's successful is that _____
(Give another reason why this company/product/name/ad is successful)

_____.

For example, _____.
(Give a specific example that supports the reason)

B. Now write your own paragraphs. Write one paragraph about what international marketers need to do to succeed and another on a successful ad, company, or product. Try to include words and expressions from this chapter in your paragraphs.

C. Write more paragraphs about international marketing and culture. Use five words and expressions from this chapter and your Internet research. Choose from the following topics.

▶ Describe an international company that you think does a good job of selling its products in your culture. Explain why you think they are successful.

▶ Describe an ad (either a print ad or a TV ad) that you like and explain why you like it.

▶ Compare two ads for the same product.

▶ Use your own idea.

On Your Own

Project

Design an ad. Work in small groups. Design a print ad for 18- to 24-year-olds in your country or culture, or a country or culture of your choice.

Choose one of the following products and give it a name (brand it).

▶ A computer or other technology product for college students

▶ A music CD

▶ An article of clothing

▶ A food or drink

▶ Your own idea

Step 1: Practice

Work with your group. Discuss the following issues:

▶ What will the ad look like? What images will it have? Describe them and try to draw them.

▶ What will the ad say? Write down the words for the ad.

Step 2: Design Your Ad

Now design your ad. Use the space below or a separate piece of paper. Then show it to the class. Describe the product, the target market, and the countries or cultures where you will sell it.

Step 3: Follow-Up

Evaluate your classmates' ads. Are they effective? Why or why not?

Wrap Up

How Much Do You Remember?

Check your new knowledge. In this chapter you learned facts, words, and expressions. You also learned reading skills and you practiced writing. Complete the following to check what you remember.

1. What does a branding consultant do? _____

    _____

2. What will make an international marketer successful in different countries around the world?

    _____

    _____

3. What's a *market*? What does *to market* mean? _____

    _____

4. Use the expression *hope to sell* in a sentence. _____

    _____

5. How might you connect with this topic: marketing Italian fruit drinks in Japan? _____

    _____

6. How can you limit an Internet search? _____

    _____

Second Timed Readings

Now reread "An Interview with a Branding Consultant" and "International Marketing: Strategies for Success." Time each reading separately. Write your times in the Timed Reading Chart on page 236.

Crossword Puzzle

Complete the crossword puzzle to practice some words and expressions from this chapter.

CLUES

Across ➡

3. The color green has negative _____ in Malaysia
7. People who buy things
8. What will make Japanese consumers _____ _____ _____ a new juice drink?
9. Ideas about what is important and how to behave
10. Being alike

Down ⬇

1. A company that makes a product
2. Study carefully
4. "It won't leak in your pocket and embarrass you!" is one of these.
5. This is what companies want from their customers.
6. A company that operates stores

What is Physical Science?

Science is often divided into two areas: physical science and life science. Astronomy, chemistry, earth science, geophysics, optics, and physics are all physical sciences. There are many interesting areas in physical science to study, such as:

- asteroids
- black holes
- climatology
- earthquakes
- X-rays

The father of astronomy is Tyco Brahe. He discovered a supernova in 1572. He did not accept the Copernicus model of the universe, so he thought the stars revolved around the earth, which did not move.

SOME FAMOUS PHYSICAL SCIENTISTS

Tyco Brahe—Danish astronomer, 1546–1601

William Maclure—American geologist, 1763–1840

Annie Jump Cannon—American astronomer, 1863–1941

Dorothy Crowfoot Hodgkin—English chemist and X-ray crystallographer; Noble Laureate, 1910–1994

Irene Joliot-Curie—French chemist; Nobel laureate 1887–1956

Verner Sunomi—American meteorologist, 1915–1995

Kenichi Fukui—Japanese chemist; Nobel Laureate, 1918–1998

Physical Science and You

People who study physical science work in engineering, medicine, meteorology, space exploration, computer science, and industry.

Do you want to study physical science? Ask yourself these questions:

- Am I curious about how things work?
- Do I like to think about problems and solutions?
- Do I like to do experiments?
- Do I like mathematics?

7 Mars

> The creative conquest of space will serve as a wonderful substitute for war. 🔔
>
> —*James S. McDonnell (American builder of the Mercury and Gemini space capsules, 1899–1980)*

CHAPTER PREVIEW

In this chapter, you'll:

Content
▶ find out how the planet Mars has influenced various cultures
▶ learn about the geography of Mars

Reading Skills
▶ use pictures and captions to preview a reading
▶ use Greek and Latin word parts to guess the meanings of words

Vocabulary Skills
▶ use words and expressions to discuss the influence of Mars on everyday life
▶ use words and expressions to talk about space exploration and the geography of Mars
▶ use expressions to make comparisons

Writing Skills
▶ write about works of science fiction and express an opinion about space exploration

Internet Skills
▶ limit and focus an Internet search

SHORT SURVEY

In my opinion, space exploration is:

❑ extremely important

❑ somewhat important

❑ not important at all

❑ not important today, but perhaps in the future

❑ other _____

Reading 1:

What are some ways that Mars has influenced people around the world? Read "Mars and the Human Imagination" to find out.

Reading 2:

What are some of the great mysteries about Mars? "The Geology of Mars" has some of the answers.

What do you think?

In my culture . . .

That's interesting. In my culture we . . .

Answer the following questions. Compare your answers with a partner.

The Planets and You

1. What are some fairy tales or myths in your culture about the solar system (the planets, the moon, the stars, and the sun)? _____

   _____

   Tell your partner about one.

2. List the names of the nine planets in English. _____

   _____

3. Give the planet names in your native language. Say or write them for your partner. Where do the planet names in your native language come from? That is, what is the source of the planet names in your native language? (In English, most of the planets get their names from Roman gods.) _____

   _____

4. What associations do the planets, sun, stars, and moon have in your native language? That is, when you hear the names, what do you think of? (For example, some people associate the moon with romance.) Are the associations negative or positive?

   _____

   _____

   _____

   _____

Reading 1: Mars and the Human Imagination

Before You Read

Preview

A. The title of Reading 1 is "Mars and the Human Imagination." What kind of information might the reading include? Discuss your ideas with a partner.

B. Think about science fiction books, movies, or TV programs that you have read or seen about space travel and aliens (beings from space). You do not need to remember the exact title. Next, answer the following questions: Is the story realistic? Explain your answer. Are the aliens friendly or frightening? Describe them. Use the following chart.

Title of Book, Movie, or TV Program (if you know it)	Realistic?	Aliens: Friendly or Frightening?
Starship Troopers	Story wasn't realistic, but the human characters were.	Frightening. Aliens were giant, scary bugs.

C. Now discuss your answers from the chart with your partner.

I saw *Starship Troopers*. It was . . .

I saw . . .

Vocabulary

Here are some words and expressions from "Mars and the Human Imagination." Complete each sentence below with the correct word or expression.

conflicts	inspired	invaders	make observations about	panic
reflects	themes	threatening	warrior	

1. The alien in the movie *E.T.* isn't frightening or _____; on the contrary, he's very friendly and nice.

2. Many cultures have a _____ god who represents war and fighting.

3. The two nations had many _____ in the past, but today they are at peace. They have not had any fights in several years.

4. Scientists _____ _____ _____ the planets using sophisticated equipment. People in ancient civilizations got information about the planets simply by looking at them.

5. *E.T.*, a science fiction movie from the 1980s, _____ the positive ideas that many people had about technology and space exploration at that time. Unlike in the 1950s and the 1960s, they were excited about things that were new and unfamiliar.

6. The sun, moon, stars and planets have _____ many poems, books, and songs. Poets, writers, and musicians have often gotten ideas from observing the skies.

7. The ideas and feelings that authors communicate are called _____. Sometimes they state these ideas directly and sometimes they don't.

8. Many works of science fiction show aliens as evil _____ who come to Earth with the intention of taking control of the planet.

9. Many people felt _____ when they heard the frightening news report. This sudden fear led to many deaths and accidents.

As You Read

As you read, think about this question:

▶ How has Mars influenced people in different places and times?

 Mars and the Human Imagination

People have always been both fascinated and frightened by the planet Mars, perhaps because of its unmistakable red color. Since ancient times, Mars—also known as "The Red Planet"—has influenced mythology, literature, movies, and daily life.

Mars in the Ancient World

The Babylonians, who studied astronomy as early as 400 B.C., were one of the first cultures
5 to make observations about the planet Mars. The Babylonians named the planet *Nergal*—the great hero, the king of conflicts. The Egyptians also made observations about the planets. They called Mars *Har Decher*—the Red One. The Greeks called the planet *Ares* after their god of war, while the Romans called it *Mars,* their name for the same god. The ancient Chinese named the planet *Huoxing,* the "Fire Star," and as in Western cultures, Chinese mythology
10 showed Mars as a powerful, red-faced warrior.

Literature

Mars has inspired writers throughout time. English novels about Mars include *Gulliver's Travels,* written in 1726 by the Irish writer Jonathan Swift. In it, Swift refers to two moons orbiting Mars. These moons were actually not discovered until 1877. Twenty years later, in 1897, the English writer H.G. Wells wrote *The War of the Worlds,* a story about technologically
15 advanced Martians invading Earth. The novel reflects the negative feelings that people had about technology during the industrial age (the late 1800s) in Europe. *The Martian Chronicles,* written in 1951 by the American author Ray Bradbury, presents the opposite idea of Martians as threatening aliens. In it, humans are the evil invaders of Mars. Bradbury's novel reflects one of the themes of mid-20th century science fiction: human weaknesses.

Radio and Movies

20 The Red Planet has also influenced popular media such as radio and movies. For example, the American actor and director Orson Welles wrote a radio play version of H.G. Wells' *The War of the Worlds.* Broadcast on October 30, 1938, the play caused extensive panic throughout

the United States. Before the performance, Welles introduced the play and said that it was fiction. However, the realistic style of the program, which included news bulletins and on-the-spot reporting, convinced many listeners that the invasion was actually happening.

Other movies about Mars include "Flash Gordon: Mars Attacks the World" (1938), a film in which Martians who look like humans try to conquer Earth. In "The Angry Red Planet" (1959), astronauts fight against various alien beings on Mars, such as a giant spider. In "Planet of Blood" (1966), a Martian vampire is brought to Earth. More recently, in "Mission to Mars" (2000), astronauts on Mars discover that human life began on that planet.

Daily Life

Mars has also influenced the names of the days of the week. Tuesday gets its name from the ancient Babylonians. To the Babylonians, "Mars Day" was Tuesday. They were the first to divide the week into seven days. Each day was named for one of the heavenly bodies: the sun, the moon, Mars, Mercury, Venus, Jupiter, and Saturn. They believed that these objects influenced people's lives on the days that were named for them. Because Mars is red, the Babylonians associated Mars with aggression and performed special ceremonies on Tuesdays to avoid the negative influence of the warlike planet.

Mars Day is still Tuesday in several languages: *Mardi* (French), *Martedi* (Italian), *Martes* (Spanish). *Tuesday* in English may not seem as though it's related to Mars. However, the English borrowed "Tews" from their Norse invaders' god of war, Tyr, and eventually "Tewsday" became *Tuesday.*

Word Count: 568

Source: *Planet Mars in Popular Culture* (NASA)

Timed Reading

Read "Mars and the Human Imagination" again. Read at a comfortable speed. Time your reading.

Start time: _____

End time: _____

My reading time: _____

After You Read

Comprehension

A. Fill in the bubble of the sentence that best describes the main idea of "Mars and the Human Imagination."

    (A) Both the Romans and the Greeks named Mars after the god of war.

    (B) Mars has influenced and inspired people from ancient times to the present.

    (C) Most stories and movies about Mars and Martians are realistic.

B. Fill in the bubble for each correct answer.

1. Which statement is correct?

    (A) Many ancient civilizations had similar ideas about the planet Mars.

    (B) Most ancient civilizations did not see Mars in the same way.

    (C) No ancient civilizations studied the sky or the planets.

2. *The Martian Chronicles* shows _____ as threatening.

    (A) Martians   (B) humans   (C) humans and Martians

3. In October of 1938, many people thought that Martians were invading Earth because _____.

    (A) they read H.G. Well's *The War of the Worlds*

    (B) they heard a news report about a real invasion

    (C) they heard a radio play about an invasion that sounded real

4. "Mars Day" in English is _____.

    (A) Thursday   (B) Monday   (C) Tuesday

5. The red color of Mars has made many civilizations associate it with _____.

    (A) heat   (B) aggression   (C) love

Talk About It

Discuss the following questions in small groups.

1. What influences has Mars had on your culture or native language?

2. Do you believe that there is life on other planets? Is so, what might the beings look like? If not, why not?

Reading 2: The Geology of Mars

Before You Read

Reading Skills

> ### Using Pictures and Captions to Preview
>
> Photographs, diagrams, and drawings help you understand new ideas in a reading passage. In textbooks these are often called figures. They often have captions (explanations) that give even more information. If you look at photographs, diagrams, and drawings and their captions before you read, they will help you to predict what the reading is about. If you look at the pictures and captions as you read, they will help you understand the author's ideas. Pictures and captions can also help you understand new words.

Practice

Look at the figures in "The Geology of Mars" on pages 151–153 and answer the following questions.

1. Is there a large canyon on Mars? Which figure answers this question?

   _____

2. Does Mars have polar ice caps? Which figure answers this question?

   _____

3. Are there deserts on Mars? Which figure answers this question?

   _____

4. Are there volcanoes on Mars? Which figure answers this question?

   _____

5. Are there channels on Mars? Which figure answers this question?

   _____

6. Will the reading discuss the topic of water on Mars? Which figures answers this question?

   _____

7. Now you have a pretty good idea of what "The Geology of Mars" means. What do you think the reading will be about? _____

_____

Preview

A. The title of Reading 2 is "The Geology of Mars." What are some examples of the geology of Earth? In what ways do you think the geology of Mars is similar to the geology of Earth? In what ways is it different? Discuss these questions with a partner.

B. Preview words from the reading. Look at the underlined words in the sentences. Match each one with the correct meaning. Write the letter of the correct answer on the line.

Sentences

_____ **1.** The earth turns on its <u>axis</u> once every 24 hours.

_____ **2.** The fog is <u>denser</u> today than yesterday. I can't see ahead of me.

_____ **3.** The machines were very sensitive; they <u>detected</u> things that people could not see.

_____ **4.** One day it was hot; the next day it was cold. The weather changed <u>drastically</u>.

_____ **5.** Ice is <u>evidence</u> that once there was water here.

_____ **6.** Many scientists are interested in the <u>extermination</u> of the dinosaurs. One theory is that an asteroid hit the Earth and caused their disappearance.

_____ **7.** When the rock hit the ground, the <u>impact</u> was so strong that it made a big hole.

_____ **8.** You can <u>infer</u> from his angry expression that the alien isn't happy.

_____ **9.** Earth has one moon <u>orbiting</u> around it.

_____ **10.** There are two <u>parallel</u> mountain ranges in that region that go from north to south.

Meanings

a. guess

b. crash; collision

c. moving around another object in space

d. noticed; found

e. death; extinction

f. thicker

g. an imaginary straight line on which a planet turns

h. running side by side but not touching

i. in an extreme manner

j. proof

Physics is puzzle-solving... puzzles created by nature, not by the mind of man.

—Maria Goeppert Mayer (German-American physicist, 1906–1972)

As You Read

As you read, think about this question:

▶ Why do scientists think there may have once been life on Mars?

The Geology of Mars

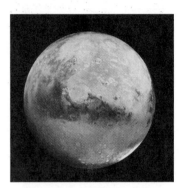

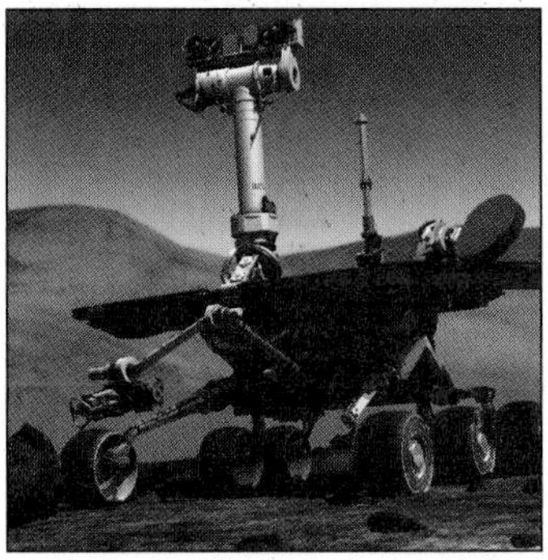

Figure 7.1: Picture of Mars made by the Hubble Space Telescope orbiting Earth

Mars, the fourth planet from the sun, has the most "Earthlike" environment of all the planets. Sometimes known as the "Red Planet" because of its reddish color, Mars shares certain physical and atmospheric features with Earth. Images from orbiting spacecraft show a world with familiar features: polar ice caps, canyons, clouds, and winds. Pictures from the spacecrafts *Mariner, Viking,* and *Mars Global Surveyor,* and from ground-based rovers such as *Spirit* and *Opportunity,* have revealed the true marvels of Mars.

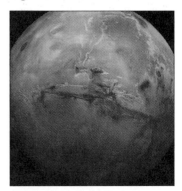

Figure 7.2: *Mars Rover* Opportunity

The Surface of Mars

Taking a look at the surface of Mars, we can see an enormous canyon, the *Valles Marineris,* that runs along the equator. This canyon, 5,000 kilometers (3,000 miles) long, 100 kilometers (62 miles) wide, and 10 kilometers (6 miles) deep, is much larger than the Grand Canyon. It is so much larger that if it were on Earth, it would stretch across the entire United States.

Mars also has polar ice caps. They vary in size depending on the season. They shrink during the summer and grow during the winter. For example, the southern cap, consisting of frozen carbon dioxide, covers a region in winter of about 5,900 km (about 3,600 miles) in diameter. Despite their size, the Martian polar caps contain very little water, far less, for example, than the ice caps of our own planet. Martian "winters" and "summers" result from the tilt of its rotation axis, in the same way that our cycle of seasons is caused by the Earth's rotation axis. However, Martian seasons are more extreme than Earth's because its atmosphere is less dense than Earth's. The less dense atmosphere of Mars does not retain heat as well as the atmosphere of Earth.

Figure 7.3: *The Valles Marineris, the Grand Canyon of Mars*

The Martian poles are bordered by extensive deserts with dunes. Martian winds blow these dunes into parallel ridges. Much

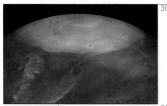

Figure 7.4: The north Martian polar cap (A) and the south Martian polar cap (B)

Figure 7.6: Dune fields in the Martian desert

further from the poles, closer to the equator, is a region called Tharsis, which contains several peaks. One, the Olympus Mons, is 25 kilometers (about 16 miles) high, nearly three times the height of Earth's highest peaks.

Astrogeologists believe that the Tharsis region formed as hot material rose from deep inside the planet and forced the surface upward as it reached the crust. The hot matter then erupted through the crust and formed volcanoes. Some planetary geologists think that this may have also created the Valles Marineris; they think it may have formed as the Tharsis region swelled and stretched, making a big crack in the crust. Others think that the Valles Marineris is evidence that Mars has tectonic activity—earthquakes—just like Earth.

Perhaps the most surprising features that were revealed by the Viking spacecraft are the huge channels and dry riverbeds, such as those seen in Figure 7.7. More recently, images of the surface of Mars from the rover Opportunity showed grooves in rocks that were formed by the presence of water. The rover also detected large amounts of

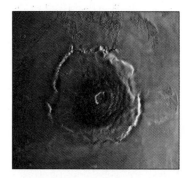

Figure 7.5: The two volcanoes in the Tharsis region

hematite, a mineral that forms in a wet environment. Scientists infer from this evidence that liquid water once flowed on Mars, even though there is no water present now. In fact, many scientists believe that huge lakes and small oceans once existed on Mars. The creates a big question: Where did the water go? A look at the atmosphere of Mars reveals the answer to this mystery.

The Atmosphere of Mars

Clouds and wind-blown dust are visible evidence that Mars has an atmosphere. Analyses of the atmosphere show that it is mostly carbon dioxide (95%) with small amounts of nitrogen (3%), oxygen, and water. Astronomers have measured the density of the atmosphere and have found that it is very low—only about 1% the density of Earth's atmosphere. Its density is so low that it cannot trap heat. This, and the fact that Mars is far from the Sun, make the planet very cold. The average temperature is 218 Kelvin (−67 F). So, although water exists on Mars,

Figure 7.7: Channels probably made by running water on Mars

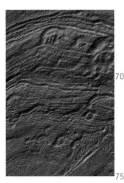

Figure 7.8: *Martian rock etched (cut) by water. Image credit: NASA/JPL/Cornell/ASU*

most of it is frozen—either on the surface of the planet as permafrost (ground that is always frozen) or in the polar caps. Clouds of dry ice (frozen CO_2) and water-ice crystals (H_2O) drift over Mars, but no rain falls from the Martian sky because the atmosphere is too cold and it contains too little water.

The existence of channels, minerals such as hematite, and grooved rocks are evidence that in the past, Mars was warmer, had a denser atmosphere, and therefore, water was present. However, scientists think that milder climate ended billions of years ago. But there is the persistent question: Where did the water go?

One explanation is that some water may lie buried below the Martian surface as ice. If the Martian climate was once warmer and then cooled drastically, water could have condensed from its atmosphere and frozen. It might have formed sheets of ice. Wind might have buried these sheets under layers of dust, the same as in polar and mountain regions on Earth. So, Mars' water may now be mostly subsurface ice. Which leads to another question: Why did the planet cool off?

According to one theory, a huge asteroid (a rock that orbits the Sun) may have struck Mars. The impact might have blasted its atmosphere into space. Although this is rare, something similar happened on Earth. About 65 million years ago, an asteroid hit Earth, and this may have led to the extermination of the dinosaurs. Another explanation is that Mars' low gravity caused gas molecules to escape over the first 1 to 2 billion years of the planet's history.

Whatever the reasons for the changes in Mars' atmosphere, the presence of water has always made scientists curious about the possibility of past life on the planet. Continuing research may someday reveal whether such a scenario could have existed.

Word Count: 892

Source: *Explorations: An Introduction to Astronomy* (Arny)

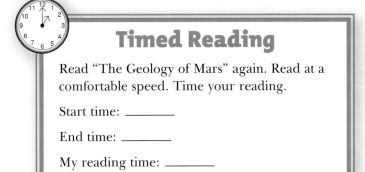

Timed Reading

Read "The Geology of Mars" again. Read at a comfortable speed. Time your reading.

Start time: _____

End time: _____

My reading time: _____

After You Read

Main Idea

Which sentence best describes the main idea of "The Geology of Mars"? Fill in the bubble of the correct answer.

- (A) Explorations of the surface and the atmosphere of Mars show that the planet is colder and drier than Earth.

- (B) Explorations of the surface and the atmosphere of Mars show a strange and extreme environment where there is no possibility of life.

- (C) Explorations of the surface and the atmosphere of Mars show similarities with Earth and the possibility of life in the past.

Getting the Details

A. Fill in the bubble for each correct answer.

1. Why are seasons on Mars more extreme than seasons on Earth?

   - (A) Because the polar caps on Mars are larger than the polar caps on Earth.
   - (B) Because the atmosphere of Mars is less dense than the atmosphere of Earth.
   - (C) Because Mars doesn't have the same position on its axis as Earth does.

2. Why do scientists think that water once existed on Mars?

   - (A) There are channels and dry riverbeds on the surface of Mars.
   - (B) There are grooves in rocks found on the surface of Mars.
   - (C) Both A and B

3. Which statement is true?

   - (A) Mars is very cold because it's far from the Sun, and its atmosphere is not very dense.
   - (B) Mars is very cold because its atmosphere has small amounts of oxygen and water.
   - (C) Mars is very cold because most of its surface is frozen.

4. A denser atmosphere means that a planet is _____ .

   - (A) colder   (B) wetter   (C) warmer

5. Scientists are interested in finding evidence of water on Mars because it could prove that there _____ .

    Ⓐ may be life on Mars in the future

    Ⓑ was life on Mars in the past

    Ⓒ never was life on Mars

Reading Skills

Guessing Meaning Using Latin and Greek Roots

You can often guess the meaning of a new word by looking at its context (the words around it). You can also guess the meanings of words by analyzing their roots. This is especially true for scientific words, which are often combinations of roots from Greek and Latin. These Greek and Latin word parts are used over and over again in science. If you know a few of them, you can guess many new words. Here are a few Greek and Latin word parts that appear in words in this chapter.

Word Part	Meaning	Word Part	Meaning
astro/aster	stars	nom	law, science
geo	earth	oid	like
hema	blood	ology	study of
ite	like	sub	under

Practice

Read these sentences from Reading 1 and Reading 2 and answer the questions about the underlined words. Use the information about Greek and Latin word parts to help you.

1. Astrogeologists believe that the Tharsis region formed as hot material rose from deep inside the planet.

What do astrogeologists do? _____

2. The Babylonians, who studied astronomy as early as 400 B.C., were one of the first cultures to make observations about the planet Mars.

What is astronomy? _____

3. The rover also detected large amounts of hematite, a mineral that forms in a wet environment.

What does hematite look like? _____

4. So, Mars' water may now be mostly <u>subsurface</u> ice.

Where is the water that turned to ice on Mars? _____

5. About 65 million years ago, an <u>asteroid</u> hit Earth, and this may have led to the extermination of the dinosaurs.

What's an asteroid? _____

Vocabulary

A. Here are some more words and expressions from "The Geology of Mars." Find them in the reading and circle them.

B. Now match each one with the correct underlined word or expression in a sentence. Write the letter of the word or expression next to the sentence that contains its match.

Noun	Verbs	
a. tilt	b. are bordered by	e. rose from
	c. consisting of	f. runs along
	d. drift over	

_____ **1.** Long ago, hot material <u>moved upward from</u> deep inside the planet. This event created a mountain range.

_____ **2.** Unlike Mars, the poles on Earth <u>are</u> not <u>next to</u> deserts. In fact, deserts are thousands of miles from either pole.

_____ **3.** The clouds on Mars, <u>which contain</u> mostly dry ice and water, do not produce rain.

_____ **4.** The clouds on Mars <u>fly slowly over</u> the planet, but do not produce rain.

_____ **5.** An enormous canyon on Mars <u>travels along</u> its equator.

_____ **6.** The <u>slant</u> of the Earth on its axis causes the different seasons.

Expressions

Comparison Expressions

"The Geology of Mars" contains several expressions used to make comparisons. Some express differences; others express similarities.

Differences
is/are more . . . than
is/are less . . . than
is/are (much) . . . -er than

Similarities
the same as
just like

Examples:
Mars is smaller than Earth.
Just like Earth, Mars has deserts.

Practice

A. Find and underline the comparison expressions from the box above in "The Geology of Mars."

B. Now use some of them to complete the sentences about the following facts. (Note: You may use some expressions more than once.)

1. **Facts:** Olympus Mons is about 16 miles high. Mt. Everest is about 5.5 miles high.

   Comparison: Olympus Mons _____ _____ _____ Mt. Everest.

2. **Facts:** The Valles Marineris is 3,000 miles long. The Grand Canyon is about 2,000 miles long.

   Comparison: The Valles Marineris _____ _____ _____ the Grand Canyon.

3. **Facts:** Mars has polar caps. Earth has polar caps.

   Comparison: Mars has polar ice caps _____ _____ Earth.

4. **Facts:** Sheets of ice are buried under dust on Mars. Sheets of ice are buried under dust on Earth.

   Comparison: Sheets of ice are buried under dust on Mars, _____ _____

   _____ on Earth.

Internet Research

Focusing Your Search

In Chapter 6, you combined keywords and used quotation marks to limit a search. You can also limit a search by using a minus sign in front of a keyword that you want to eliminate. The minus sign subtracts a topic to make a search more specific. For example, let's say you want to find out about the geology of *Venus*. The keyword *Venus* is too general. *Venus geology* will give you too many results, too. You will also get too many results with *Venus surface atmosphere*. However, if you use *Venus surface −atmosphere* you will get fewer, more precise results. After you get information about the surface, you can search again for *Venus atmosphere −surface*. This way, each time your search is focused on what you want.

Practice

Practice combining keywords, using quotations, and using the minus sign to limit and focus a search. Find information about the geology of Mars or of other planets. First, use general terms. Then combine keywords or put quotations around keyword combinations. Finally, try eliminating results using the minus sign. Compare your results with a partner's.

Try using the following keywords or use your own:

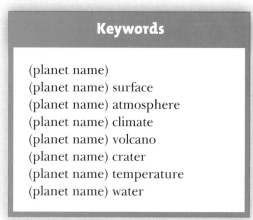

Keywords
(planet name)
(planet name) surface
(planet name) atmosphere
(planet name) climate
(planet name) volcano
(planet name) crater
(planet name) temperature
(planet name) water

Note: The minus sign (−) is especially good for eliminating non-scientific information from a search about the planets. For example, what is the difference between a search for *Mars* and a search for *Mars −candy*?

Write About It

A. Write the following paragraphs. Fill in the blanks. Write complete sentences.

Paragraph One

My favorite _____ about _____
(Write *book, movie,* or *TV program*)   (Write *space, space exploration, Mars* or *aliens*)

is_____ . I like it because _____
(Give the title)   (Give one reason why you like it)

_____ .

For example, _____ .
(Give an example that illustrates this reason)

It's also my favorite because _____
(Give another reason why you like it)

_____ .

For example, _____ .
(Give an example that illustrates this reason)

Paragraph Two

In my opinion, space exploration is _____ for three reasons. First of all,
(Write *important* or *not important*)

_____
(Give one reason for your opinion)

_____ .

For example, _____ .
(Give an example that illustrates this reason)

In addition, _____
(Give a second reason for your opinion)

_____ .

For example, _____ .
(Give an example that illustrates this reason)

Finally, _____
(Give a third reason for your opinion)

_____ .

For example, _____ .
(Give an example that illustrates this reason)

B. Now write your own paragraphs. Write one paragraph on your favorite science fiction book, movie, or TV program. Write a second on the importance of space exploration. Try to include words and expressions from this chapter in your paragraphs.

C. Write more paragraphs about science fiction, Mars, other planets, and space exploration. Use five words and expressions from this chapter and your Internet research. Choose from the following topics.

▶ Compare the geology of two planets.

▶ Compare two books or movies about space or aliens.

▶ Would you like to travel in space? Why or why not? Who would you like to go with? Why?

▶ Use your own idea.

On Your Own

Project

Take a survey. Ask your classmates their opinions of space exploration.

Step 1: Practice

Listen as your teacher reads the survey questions. Do you understand them?
Repeat them with your teacher so you can pronounce them.

Step 2: Take a Survey

Ask three classmates their opinions of space exploration. Fill in the following chart.

Space Exploration Survey

Person 1: _____

1. Is space exploration a good idea? ____ Yes ____ No
2. Why or why not?
   Answer: _____.

Person 2: _____

1. Is space exploration a good idea? ____ Yes ____ No
2. Why or why not?
   Answer: _____.

Person 3: _____

1. Is space exploration a good idea? ____ Yes ____ No
2. Why or why not?
   Answer: _____.

Step 3: Follow-Up

Explain the results of your survey to the class. What do most people think? Are there any similarities in the reasons people gave for their opinions? Is there a difference in opinions between males and females? Were you surprised by any of the answers? Why or why not?

Wrap Up

How Much Do You Remember?

Check your new knowledge. In this chapter you learned facts, words, and expressions. You also learned reading skills and you practiced writing. Complete the following to check what you remember.

1. Give three examples of the ways in which Mars has influenced culture and everyday life.

_____

_____

2. Give one similarity and one difference between the geology of Mars and the geology of Earth.

_____

_____

3. How can pictures and captions help you preview a reading passage?

_____

_____

4. Give a word that has the Latin word part *astro* and explain what it means. _____

_____

5. Use *evidence* in a sentence. _____

_____

6. Use *just like* in a sentence. _____

_____

7. How can the minus sign (−) help you in an Internet search? _____

_____

Second Timed Readings

Now reread "Mars and the Human Imagination" and "The Geology of Mars." Time each reading separately. Write your times in the Timed Reading Chart on page 237.

Crossword Puzzle

Complete the crossword puzzle to practice some words and expressions from this chapter.

CLUES

Across →
1. An imaginary line that runs through the center of a planet
5. Thicker
9. In an extreme way
10. Guess

Down ↓
2. The sun, the planets, and the moon
3. Shows
4. What the Earth is doing right now around the Sun
6. Proof
7. Next to, but not crossing
8. Creatures from outer space

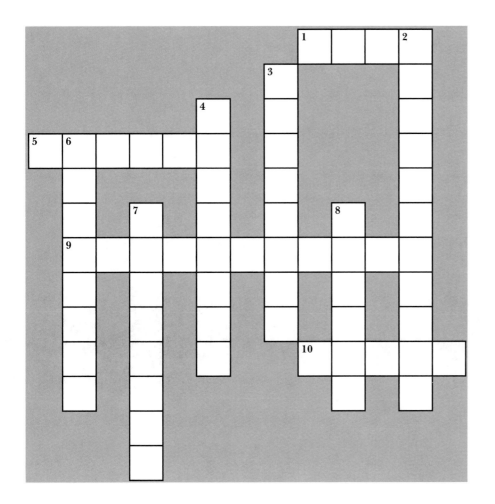

8 Meteorology

CHAPTER PREVIEW

In this chapter, you'll:

Content
▶ learn what to do in a weather emergency
▶ learn about the tools that meteorologists use to predict the weather

Reading Skills
▶ preview by combining strategies
▶ locate keywords in a reading

Vocabulary Skills
▶ use words and expressions to describe weather and weather predictions
▶ talk about the weather and weather emergencies using verb phrases

Writing Skills
▶ compare the weather in two places
▶ discuss the kinds of weather that you like

Internet Skills
▶ find information about weather on the Internet

> Weather lovers are part scientist, part poet. ᐅ♦
>
> —*T. Morris Longstreth (American author, 1886–1975)*

SHORT SURVEY

I get weather information:

❑ from the newspaper

❑ from the radio

❑ from TV

❑ from the Internet

❑ by looking out the window

❑ other _____

Reading 1:

Do you know what to do in a weather emergency? Read "Weather-Related Emergencies" to find out.

Reading 2:

How do meteorologists know what the weather will be? Read "How Weather Prediction Works" to find out.

What do you think?

Complete the following sentences. Compare your answers with a partner.

The Weather and You

What do you like to do in different types of weather? Do you like to do outdoor activities? Do you like to stay inside? Answer for yourself and then compare your answers with a partner. (If you've never experienced a certain type of weather, explain what you *would* like to do if you were in this weather.)

Examples:

When it's raining, I _like to take a long walk_____.

When it's very cold, I _usually stay inside_____.

When it's sunny, I _____.

When it's raining, I _____.

When it snows, I _____
_____.

When it's foggy, I _____
_____.

When it's windy, I _____
_____.

When it's very cold, I _____
_____.

When it's warm, I _____
_____.

When it's very hot, I _____
_____.

Reading 1: Weather-Related Emergencies

Before You Read

Preview

A. The title of Reading 1 is "Weather-Related Emergencies." What's a "weather-related emergency"? Try to think of at least three examples. Discuss your ideas with a partner.

B. How prepared are you for different kinds of weather? Do you know what to do in extreme weather conditions? Answer the following questions and compare your answers with your partner.

1. When was the last time you saw lightning? _____

2. Do you know anyone who has been hit by lightning?   Yes   No

    If yes, what happened? _____

    _____

3. When was the last heavy rain where you live? _____

4. Do you know anyone whose home was flooded because of heavy rains?   Yes   No

    If yes, what happened? _____

    _____

5. Do you know what to do during lightning?   Yes   No

    A flood?   Yes   No

    A sandstorm?   Yes   No

    a. When there's lightning, you should _____.

    b. When there's a flood, you should _____.

    c. When there's a sandstorm, you should _____.

Vocabulary

Preview these words from "Weather-Related Emergencies." Match each one with its correct meaning. Write the letter of the correct answer on the line.

Words	Meanings
_____ **1.** bounce	**a.** giving new energy to
_____ **2.** struck by	**b.** usually
_____ **3.** flagpole	**c.** covered structures
_____ **4.** grains	**d.** in an unplanned way; unintentionally
_____ **5.** inadvertently	**e.** live; stay alive
_____ **6.** outlets	**f.** hit by
_____ **7.** exhilarating	**g.** places to plug in electrical devices
_____ **8.** shelters	**h.** small, hard, round pieces of something
_____ **9.** survive	**i.** go up and down after hitting a surface
_____ **10.** typically	**j.** a tall support for a flag

> **Every sky has its beauty.** ❧
>
> —*George Gissing (English novelist and essayist, 1857–1903)*

As You Read

As you read, think about this question:

▶ What should you do if you are in lightning, a flood, or a sandstorm?

🎧 Weather-Related Emergencies

"Sunshine is delicious, rain is refreshing, wind braces us, snow is exhilarating; there really is no such thing as bad weather, only different kinds of good weather," said John Ruskin, an English writer and critic. However, people caught in dangerous weather conditions may not agree. It's wise, in fact, to know what to do in case of very bad weather—weather emergencies. Here are some tips on how to survive weather disasters.

Lightning

Right now, about 2,000 thunderstorms are occurring on earth and lightning is striking the ground about 100 times per second. Although most people who are struck by lightning survive, it's better *not* to be hit. Here's what you can do to avoid being struck by lightning.

Lightning

If you're outdoors, stay low—away from open fields or tops of mountains. If you are in an open area, get down but put as little of your body on the ground as possible; don't lie flat. If you can, stand on your backpack, or whatever you have with you that does not conduct electricity (such as plastic). Avoid a tree by itself, rain, and picnic shelters. Do not stand near metal objects such as flagpoles or metal fences. If you are swimming, get out of the water. If you're in a car, stay in the car, but don't touch any metal surface. Keep the windows rolled up.

If you're inside, avoid touching anything in contact with the outside such as the shower or sink, a metal door, or a window frame. Also, don't touch electrical outlets and electrical devices such as the telephone, a computer, or the television (especially TVs with cable).

Floods

Rainstorms can cause floods. Lightning and floods are the greatest causes of weather-related death and injury in many places around the world. It's surprising how little water can cause death. Here are some tips for surviving a flood.

If you're outside, State Farm Insurance suggests getting inside as quickly as possible, or go to a high place such as a

A Flood

hill or mountain. It takes only six inches of water at a speed of ten miles per hour to sweep
you off your feet, and floodwater typically runs at ten miles an hour. It's the same if you're in
a car: find a high place and get out of your car because most deaths during a flood occur in
automobiles.

If you're inside, watch out for snakes and other animals that may look for safety in your
house.

Sandstorms

Sandstorms occur when wind causes grains of sand to bounce across the surface of the
earth. Many sand and dust storms originate in the dry regions of northern China and
Mongolia and blow across the Korean peninsula and Japan.
Today, they occur five times as often as they did in the 1950s.
Here are some tips for surviving a sandstorm.

A Sandstorm

If you're outside, put a piece of wet cloth over your nose
and mouth. Put a little petroleum jelly inside your nose. If
you're in a group, link arms and stay together. If you have a
rope, attach yourselves to the rope so you won't get separated
and can keep track of anyone who gets injured. If you're in a
car, get off the road, stop the car, turn off the lights, and set
the emergency brake. Keep your lights off so cars approach-
ing you don't get confused and inadvertently drive off the road and hit your parked car. If
you're inside, just stay there until the storm is over.

The radio, television, and the safety section of your telephone book all have helpful tips
for surviving a weather-related emergency. It's important to be prepared for weather emergencies. Someday you may save someone's life, or even your own.

Word Count: 620

Source: *Severe Weather Watcher Handbook* (Meteorological Service of Canada)

Timed Reading

Read "Weather-Related Emergencies" again.
Read at a comfortable speed. Time your
reading.

Start time: _____

End time: _____

My reading time: _____

After You Read

Comprehension

A. Fill in the bubble of the sentence that best describes the main idea of "Weather-Related Emergencies."

- (A) It's important to pay attention to weather conditions every day.
- (B) It's important to be prepared for weather-related emergencies.
- (C) It's important to know where you are during a weather emergency.

B. Fill in the bubble for each correct answer.

1. Most people struck by lightning _____.

   (A) do not know it   (B) do not die   (C) do not survive

2. When you are outdoors during lightning, you should avoid

   (A) open fields   (B) metal objects   (C) both A and B

3. When there is lightning, you should _____.

   (A) get out of your car   (B) stay in your car   (C) run to the top of the mountain

4. According to the passage, most deaths during a flood occur _____.

   (A) on hill tops   (B) in open fields   (C) in automobiles

5. During a sandstorm, you should _____.

   (A) put a piece of cloth over your head
   (B) attach yourself to other members of your group
   (C) stay on the road and keep your car lights on

Talk About It

Discuss the following question with a partner.
Describe the worst weather emergency you have experienced. Were you frightened?

What's the worst weather . . .

I was in a sandstorm in . . .

Reading 2: How Weather Prediction Works

Before You Read

Reading Skills

> ### Review: Combining Strategies
>
> When you are previewing a passage, it's a good idea to use more than one strategy. In Chapter 6, you saw one way to put previewing strategies together. Now that you've learned to use pictures and captions to preview a reading, you can add the skill of connecting with the topic. Connecting with the topic prepares you by bringing background information to the reading experience. Previewing pictures and captions gives you a good idea of the main ideas that the passage will cover.

Practice

Practice connecting with the topic and using pictures and captions to preview a reading passage. Look at "How Weather Prediction Works" on pages 173–175. Answer these questions. Compare your answers with a partner.

1. The topic of the reading passage is weather prediction—how weather forecasters predict the weather. What questions can you ask yourself to connect to the topic?

   _____

2. Look at the title. What topics do you think the passage might cover?

   _____

3. Look at Figure 1 and read the caption. Why might weather prediction be important?

   _____

4. Look at Figure 2 and read the caption. If you look out the window to predict the weather, for about how long will your prediction be accurate?

   _____

5. Look at Figure 3 and read the caption. In which direction does wind travel in the United

   States? _____

6. Look at Figure 4 and read the caption. Where do East Coast snowstorms come from?

   _____

Preview

Preview these words and expressions from the reading. Complete each of the sentences below with the correct word or expression.

> chances are   climate   data   interpolation
> persistence   recognizable   trend   weather fronts

1. On a beautiful sunny day, five-year-old Nancy's _____ was rewarded. She asked her mother 15 times to go to the beach, and her mother finally said "yes."

2. Many areas of science and mathematics, such as meteorology and calculus, use _____. This means using what you know to guess at what you don't know.

3. David has lived in Peru long enough to find _____ patterns in the weather. For example, he knows that the "El Nino" weather pattern comes every three to four years.

4. Warm and cold _____ _____ cause changes in the weather. Wind makes air move around the earth. Cold air may replace warm air in an area or warm air may replace cold air.

5. If you see dark clouds and lightning, _____ _____ you will hear thunder. It's also possible that it will rain.

6. _____ is weather patterns over days, weeks, seasons, and years of time. It helps forecasters predict weather effectively.

7. Because of global warming, there is a _____ towards warmer weather everywhere in the world. In other words, the weather is gradually changing.

8. We have collected a lot of _____ about rainfall in our region over the last five years. We know how many inches of rain there is per day, month, and season. Even with all this information, we were very surprised when the town flooded last month.

As You Read

As you read, think about this question:
► How does weather prediction work?

🎧 How Weather Prediction Works

A writer once said, "Everyone talks about the weather, but no one ever does anything about it." Weather is a factor in everyday life, and knowing what the weather will be like in the future is important to everyone, from pilots to gardeners to soccer players. Over time, weather forecasting has improved enormously. For example, in the famous Tri-State Tornado of 1925, 689 people were killed in Missouri, Illinois, and Indiana. By contrast, improvements in weather prediction meant that a huge tornado that went through Oklahoma and Kansas in 1999 killed only 43 people. We all depend on weather forecasting (prediction), but how is it done and how accurate is it?

Figure 1: Accurate weather predicting saved lives in this 1999 tornado.

Weather Forecasting Techniques

There are seven different techniques used to predict the weather: persistence forecasting, trend forecasting, interpolation, steering forecasting, weather types forecasting, numerical forecasting, and climate data. The first technique, **persistence forecasting,** is based on the logical idea that the weather will remain the same as it is now. Look out the window. What is the weather like? Chances are that the weather will be the same in five minutes as it is right now. Persistence forecasting usually works well for two hours. Longer than that, changes that occur during the day must be taken into consideration.

Figure 2: Persistence Forecasting— Looking out the window will give you an accurate forecast for about the next two hours.

The second technique, **trend forecasting,** is based on the idea that weather fronts and air pressure centers will move in the future the same way as they have in the past. For

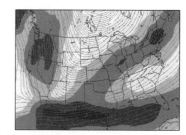

Figure 3: Wind patterns across the United States from West to East

example, if you fly from New York to California, it usually takes about six hours. If you fly from California to New York, it usually takes about five and a half hours. The reason is that winds go from the west to the east, so you are going against the wind from New York to California and with the wind from California to New York. All weather patterns do change, however, so the challenge with trend forecasting is to predict when, how, and where the change will occur.

Interpolation, the third technique, is the method of looking at the weather in two locations and then finding the average to estimate what the weather is like in a place between those two locations. It is also done using two times instead of locations. Weather forecasters use this technique because they believe that there is a generally consistent variation in the weather between two locations or between two times.

The fourth technique is **steering forecasting.** Steering forecasting techniques are used because surface weather patterns seem to move as though they are carried by upper-level winds. In actuality, this does not really happen. What does happen is that surface patterns redevelop continually in response to the movement of the wind. We can't see this actually happening, but think of a river as an example. The water pushes leaves and sticks as it flows along. It's similar with wind. The upper air "steers" or directs winds at the surface.

Figure 4: On the American East Coast, snowstorms come from the Gulf of Mexico.

Weather types forecasting is a technique based on the idea that certain weather systems or patterns with recognizable characteristics tend to occur. For example, most major East Coast snowstorms come from the eastern Gulf of Mexico and get stronger when they get to the North Carolina coast. These are called "East Coast snowstorm" types. Forecasters who can recognize different types of storms can make more accurate predictions. At one time, many meteorologists believed that the main use of computers in weather prediction would be to refine the picking of weather types. But today computers are used to calculate (not predict!) atmospheric conditions from a basic set of equations. Someday they may be used more to predict outcomes.

Powerful computers are used for **numerical forecasting.** These computers use equations to calculate atmospheric pressure and moisture patterns. Then other programs translate that calculation into actual weather conditions at specific places. With information about humidity and temperature at certain elevations, a computer can predict the chances of rain, thunderstorms, or what the temperature will be on the ground.

Climate data includes long-term averages and extremes for given locations. For example, most places in the United States have been keeping weather data for about 125 years, and a few places have data that goes back 200 years. If, for example, in 125 years it has never been colder than 55 degrees on November 1 in a certain place, then it probably won't be colder than 55 degrees there next year.

Short-term forecasts tend to rely on persistence forecasting, while long-term forecasts rely on climate data. Neither of these involves much skill. Forecasters can do them easily. It is the intermediate times that are the hardest for forecasters. Intermediate times require forecasters to analyze the interaction between trends, weather types, and steering. In any case, knowing a little bit about how forecasters work can help us decide for ourselves how accurate their predictions will be.

Word Count: 870

Source: *Meteorology* (Danielson, Levin, and Abrams)

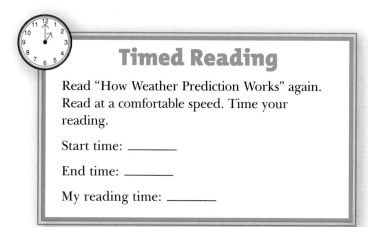

Timed Reading

Read "How Weather Prediction Works" again. Read at a comfortable speed. Time your reading.

Start time: _____

End time: _____

My reading time: _____

After You Read

Main Idea

Which sentence best describes the main idea of "How Weather Prediction Works"? Fill in the bubble of the correct answer.

Ⓐ Weather forecasters can accurately and effectively predict the weather.

Ⓑ Forecasters have many techniques that they use to help predict the weather.

Ⓒ Without computers, forecasters cannot effectively predict the weather.

Getting the Details

A. Answer the following questions about "How Weather Prediction Works."

1. Name the technique that is based on this logic: The weather will stay the way that it is now.

   _____

2. How does the wind affect travel across the United States? _____

   _____

3. With *interpolation,* weather forecasters take two different kinds of measurements. What are

   they? _____

   _____

4. Because we cannot see the wind, it is sometimes hard to understand how it affects the weather. Based on that fact, which statement is correct?

   Ⓐ Surface weather patterns redevelop in response to the movements of the winds.

   Ⓑ Surface weather patterns are carried by upper-level winds.

5. To calculate the chances of rain or the temperature on the ground, what data does a

   computer need? _____

   _____

Reading Skills

Practice

A. Read "How Weather Prediction Works" again. As you read, look for and put a star (*) next to the bolded keywords.

B. Now answer the following questions. Compare your answers with a partner.

1. How many techniques for weather prediction are described in "How Weather Prediction Works?" _____ How many of them are in bold in the article? _____

2. Explain why it takes six hours to fly from New York to California, but only five and a half hours to fly from California to New York. _____

   _____

3. Use *interpolation* to answer the following questions:

   a. James lives in Lincoln where it's 78°. Kevin lives in Madison where it's 72°. Sue lives between them in Mills. What do you estimate the temperature is in Mills? _____

   b. At 4 A.M., the temperature was 60° in Palmdale. At 10 A.M., it was 80°. What was the temperature at 7 A.M.? _____

4. Explain *climate data* in your own words. _____

_____

5. Tania is getting married in Healdsburg on June 6th. For the last 40 years, it has only rained four times on June 6th. The weather forecaster said it won't rain, but she's very worried.

What can you tell Tania? _____

_____

Vocabulary

A. Here are some more words and expressions from "How Weather Prediction Works." Find them in the reading and circle them.

Nouns	Verbs	Adjective	Gerund
atmospheric conditions factor humidity	based on redevelop taken into consideration	consistent	estimating

B. Now use some of them to complete the sentences.

1. Weather patterns change and _____ all the time. Wind is important in making this happen.

2. _____ means more than guessing; it means using the information that you have to make an *educated* guess.

3. We made our travel plans _____ _____ what you said. Your idea to go somewhere warm with lots of activities for the children seemed good to us.

4. Many people are uncomfortable in high _____. The moisture in the air makes their hair feel damp and heavy.

5. The _____ _____ are constantly changing in this region: one minute it's sunny, the next, it's cloudy.

Expressions

> ### Verbs Phrases for Talking about the Weather and Weather Emergencies
>
> Certain verb + preposition and verb + noun/pronoun + preposition combinations are useful for talking about weather.
>
> | | | |
> |---|---|---|
> | **caught in** | **keep track of** | **takes about** |
> | **require forecasters to** | **sweep you off your feet** | |
>
> **Examples:**
> If you are caught in a lightning storm, do not stand near a lone tree.
> It pays to keep track of the weather so you are prepared during an emergency.

Practice

A. Find and underline the verb phrase combinations in the box in "Weather-Related Emergencies" or "How Weather Prediction Works."

B. Now use them to complete the sentences below.

1. Fast water can _____ _____ _____ _____

   _____. This is dangerous because you might hit your head or suffer other injuries.

2. In his fifth grade class, David had to _____ _____ _____ the weather every day for a month. Then the children used email to compare their weather records with those from a class in Korea.

3. Yesterday, we were _____ _____ a bad rainstorm. We weren't expecting it and we weren't prepared.

4. Different kinds of weather_____ _____ _____ use different kinds of equipment, get different data points, and make different observations.

5. It usually _____ _____ a half hour longer to go from New York to California than from California to New York.

Internet Research

Using the Internet to Find Climate and Weather Information

The Internet is a great way to get weather information quickly. Search engines (such as google.com) and online newspapers (such as usatoday.com) are two ways to get weather information on the Internet.

If you use a search engine, you can find the weather in a particular city by using the keywords *weather Taipei*. (Note: You don't need the word "in.")

Online newspapers often have detailed weather information. If you want to find weather information in an online newspaper, go to the paper's home-page and look for a *Weather* button. The online weather page for a U.S. paper usually shows the weather for the United States; to get the weather in other parts of the world, look for a *World* or *International* button.

Practice

Practice looking for information about the weather on the Internet. Find the weather in at least three cities. Use both a search engine and at least two newspaper websites. Also, practice using the minus (−) sign to focus your search and eliminate unwanted results. Print your results and bring them to class.

Keywords

weather (city)
weather (country)
weather (region)
weather (country) –(city)
weather (region) –(country)
(place) rainfall
(place) average snowfall
(place) tornados
(place) hurricanes

Compare your results with those of your classmates.

Write About It

A. Write the following paragraphs. Fill in the blanks. Write complete sentences.

Paragraph One

On _____, the weather in _____
(Give today's date)   (Give the name of a place)

and _____ was _____.
(Give the name of another place)   (Write *very similar* or *very different*)

The weather in _____ was
(Give the name of the first place again)

_____. This was because _____
(Use a descriptive adjective: *good, bad, unpleasant*, etc.)

_____.
(Explain why the weather was this way)

The weather in _____ was _____.
(Give the name of the second place again)   (Use a descriptive adjective: *good, OK, bad*, etc.)

This was because _____

_____.

Paragraph Two

I like _____ weather. One reason that I like this type of
(Give the kind of weather you like)

weather is that_____
(Give one reason why you like this kind of weather)

_____.

For example, _____.
(Give a specific example that supports your reason)

Another reason I like it is because _____
(Give another reason why you like this kind of weather)

_____.

For example, _____.
(Give another specific example that supports your reason)

B. Now write your own paragraphs. Write one paragraph on the weather in two places and another on the type of weather that you like best. Use your Internet research and try to include words and expressions from this chapter in your paragraphs.

C. Write more paragraphs about the weather. Use five words and expressions from this chapter and your Internet research. Choose from the following topics.

▶ Describe the weather where you live now.

▶ Describe the weather where you would like to live.

▶ Explain how you protect yourself in severe weather.

▶ Explain how the weather influenced a decision about a vacation, a picnic, or another plan you had.

▶ Use your own idea.

> **My heart leaps up when I behold a rainbow.** ❧
>
> *—William Wordsworth (English poet, 1770–1850)*

On Your Own

Project

Create a world weather chart for seven international cities. Use cities where people in the class were born. If most people in your class are from the same place, add international cities to the chart to make a total of seven.

Step 1: Do Research

Use the Internet to find the high and low temperatures for each city for one month.

Step 2: Record Your Results

Add the two numbers and find the average. Use the following chart to make notes.

| Month: _____ | | | |
City	High Temperature	Low Temperature	Average
_____	_____	_____	_____
_____	_____	_____	_____
_____	_____	_____	_____
_____	_____	_____	_____
_____	_____	_____	_____
_____	_____	_____	_____
_____	_____	_____	_____

Optional: Record the average temperatures in their correct places on a map. You can find a map one in a book or on the Internet. Then copy or print it, enlarge it (make it bigger), or re-draw it.

Step 3: Follow-Up

Discuss the weather in each city. Compare the temperatures. Find the coldest place; find the hottest place. Were you surprised by any of the information? Why or why not?

Wrap Up

How Much Do You Remember?

Check your new knowledge. In this chapter you learned facts, words, and expressions. You also learned reading skills and you practiced writing. Complete the following to check what you remember.

1. What should you do if you get caught in lightning? _____

    _____

2. What does *persistence forecasting* mean? _____

3. Give an example of *climate data* forecasting. _____

    _____

4. Use *data* in a sentence. _____

    _____

5. Use *sweep you off your feet* in a sentence. _____

    _____

6. How can you identify keywords in a reading? _____

    _____

7. How can you find weather information on the Internet? _____

    _____

Second Timed Readings

Now reread "Weather-Related Emergencies" and "How Weather Prediction Works." Time each reading separately. Write your times in the Timed Reading Chart on page 237.

Crossword Puzzle

Complete the crossword puzzle to practice some words from this chapter.

CLUES

Across →
1. Small round pieces
9. Without warning
10. Information
11. It's very likely

Down ↓
2. Easy to see
3. Usually or generally
4. Stay alive
5. Weather over a period of time
6. Guessing
7. Pattern
8. It's easy to _____ _____ _____ the weather; just look out the window

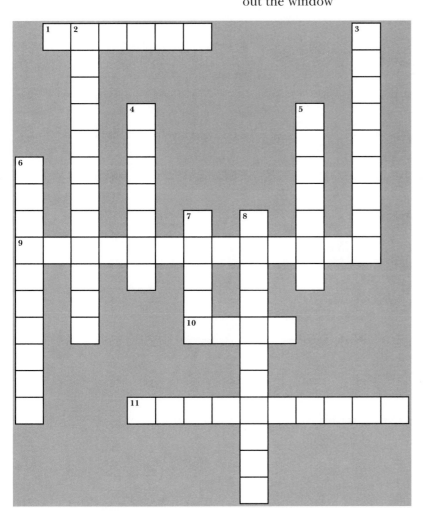

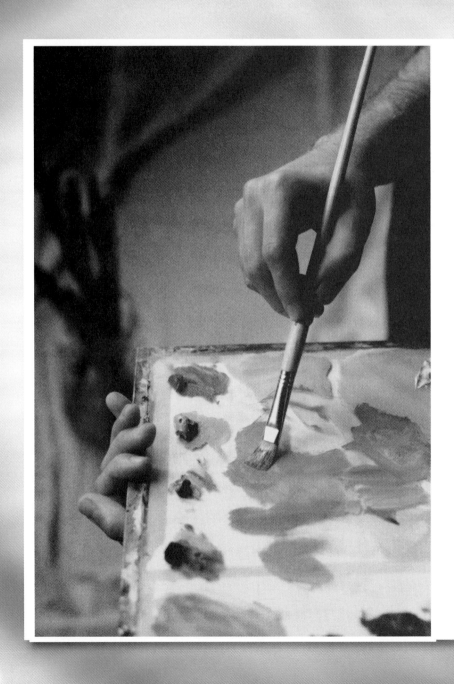

What are the Arts?

The arts include architecture, painting, photography, sculpture, dance, design, film, literature, music, and theater. Here are some additional examples of the arts:

- ceramics
- drawings
- furniture design
- novels
- operas
- performance art
- poetry
- posters
- printmaking (lithograph, engraving, etching, woodcut)
- symphonic music

The earliest humans created art. Some of the oldest works of art are cave paintings. Stone Age artists created these paintings around 15,000 B.C.

SOME PEOPLE FAMOUS IN THE ARTS

Li Po—Chinese poet, 701–762

Murasaki Shikibu—Japanese novelist, 973–1025

Leonardo di Vinci—Italian painter, 1452–1519

Thomas Chippendale—British furniture designer, 1718–1779

Wolfgang Amadeus Mozart—Austrian composer, 1756–1791

Pablo Picasso—Spanish painter, 1881–1973

Ella Fritzgerald—American jazz singer, 1917–1996

Gabriel Garcia Marquez—Colombian writer, 1928–

Anne Deveare Smith—American performance artist, 1950–

Zaha Hadid—Iraqi architect, 1950–

The Arts and You

People who study the arts work in fields such as architecture, computer graphics, teaching, filmmaking, advertising, music, and journalism. The arts are also good preparation for careers in medicine and law.

Do you want to study the arts? Ask yourself these questions:

- Do I like to perform for an audience?
- Do I like to draw or paint?
- Do I like read poetry and plays?
- Am I interested in playing or composing music?
- Do I like to design buildings or furniture?
- Do I like to make beautiful things?
- Am I creative?

CHAPTER 9 Jazz

CHAPTER PREVIEW

In this chapter, you'll:

Content
▶ learn about jazz great Duke Ellington
▶ learn about the musical traditions and cultures that influenced jazz

Reading Skills
▶ preview a passage by reading the topic sentence in each paragraph
▶ organize information about a reading by outlining it

Vocabulary Skills
▶ use words and expressions to talk about jazz and jazz artists
▶ use time expressions with prepositions

Writing Skills
▶ write about the type of music that you like
▶ write about the types of music that contributed to jazz

Internet Skills
▶ use a specialized online dictionary

> Man, if you gotta ask, you'll never know. ♪
>
> —*Louis Armstrong (American jazz musician, 1900–1971) when asked to define jazz*

SHORT SURVEY

I like to listen to music when I:

❑ study

❑ drive

❑ eat

❑ clean my room/house

❑ wash dishes

❑ other _____

Reading 1:

Why is Duke Ellington called "one of the jazz greats"? Read "A Jazz Great—Duke Ellington" to find out.

Reading 2:

What cultures and musical styles have influenced jazz? Read "About Jazz" to find out.

What do you think?

Complete the following statements. Compare your answers with a partner.

How important is music to you?

It's . . .

Music and You

1. Music is _____ to me.

    A very important   **B** somewhat important   **C** not important at all

2. I prefer _____ music.

    A hip-hop   **B** jazz   **C** techno   **D** rock   **E** classical   **F** other _____

3. There is music in my house _____ of the day.

    A 25%   **B** 50%   **C** 75%   **D** 100%

4. I prefer _____.

    A just to listen to music   **B** to dance while I listen to music

5. I have been to _____ music concerts.

    A 0   **B** 1-2   **C** 3-5   **D** over 5

6. I have been to _____ jazz festivals.

    A 0   **B** 1-2   **C** 3-5   **D** over 5

7. I buy music CDs _____.

    A once a year   **B** once a month   **C** once a week   **D** never

8. My friends and I listen to _____ types of music.

    A the same   **B** different

9. I prefer _____.

    A songs in my native language   **B** songs in English

10. My favorite musical performer is _____.

Reading 1: A Jazz Great—Duke Ellington

Before You Read

Preview

A. The title of Reading 1 is "A Jazz Great—Duke Ellington." It's about the life of an American musician. What kind of information might it include? Discuss your ideas with a partner.

B. In Reading 1 the author talks about the childhood of Duke Ellington and his later success as a bandleader. To develop your opinions about the connection between childhood influences and success, answer the questions below.

On Childhood

1. If your parents treat you as if you are very special, you will not have many long-lasting relationships in life. Do you agree or disagree? _____ Why? _____

_____

2. If your parents believe that you can "do anything," you will believe it yourself. Do you agree or disagree? _____ Why? _____

_____

On Success

1. Painting and music use different talents. If you are good at one, you probably will not be good at the other. Do you agree or disagree? _____ Why? _____

_____

2. Most successful musicians love their work and have fun with their work. Do you agree or disagree? _____ Why? _____

_____

Vocabulary

Here are some words and expressions from "A Jazz Great—Duke Ellington." Complete each sentence below with the correct word or expression.

blessed	butler	caterer	combo	instrumentalist
improvisation	mold	pampered	restrict	spoiled rotten

1. As a child, Don was _____ _____ because his parents gave him everything he wanted. Because of that, he grew up to be a very selfish person.

2. Emily wanted to be a(n) _____ and play in a band, so she asked her mother if she could learn an instrument such as the saxophone or clarinet.

3. Everyone said that Miles was _____ because he was very lucky and very talented.

4. Jeeves liked his job as a(n) _____. His responsibilities included serving drinks at parties, setting out his employer's clothes every morning, and doing small errands.

5. Harry was good at _____. He could sit down at a piano and create new songs.

6. "Don't _____ my freedom so much, Dad," said 16-year-old Chris. "All the kids are going to the club tonight and I want to go, too."

7. Jackie hired a(n) _____ to make and serve the food at her party.

8. Jackie also hired a small jazz _____ to play music. This group of musicians included a piano player, a drummer, and a bass player.

9. "I like to _____ the music to fit the musicians in the group," said Herbie, the band-leader. "If I get a good fit, we get a good sound."

10. Kathy had a(n) _____ life. She was very rich and had servants to bring her anything she wanted. She never had to go to the grocery store or take out the garbage.

As You Read

As you read, think about this question:

▶ What made Duke Ellington a jazz great?

A Jazz Great—Duke Ellington

"I'm a piano player, a rehearsal piano player, a jive-time conductor, bandleader, and sometimes I do nothing but take bows . . . and I have fun. My, my, my. My thing is having fun."

These are the words of Duke Ellington. Duke Ellington was one of the jazz greats.
5 As jazz critic Nat Hentoff said, "Ellington was a man who was an orchestra." He was an orchestra leader who successfully solved a big problem in jazz: the conflict between individual freedom and group unity within a jazz orchestra. As Ellington said:

"I regard my entire orchestra as one large instrument, and I try to play on that instrument to the fullest of its capabilities. My aim is and always has been to mold the
10 music around the man. I've found out that it doesn't matter so much what you have available, but rather what you make of what you do have—finding a good 'fit' for every instrumentalist in the group. I study each man in the orchestra and find out what he can do best, and what he would like to do."

Ellington also balanced Western European musical traditions with improvisation,
15 which was part of the African oral tradition. This combination created Ellington's well-known sound.

Born in Washington, D.C., on April 29, 1899, Edward Kennedy Ellington came from a middle-class family. He grew up in a big house not far from the White House. At that time, Washington, D.C., had the largest population of African Americans in the United
20 States, which was about one hundred thousand people. Ellington's father, James Edward Ellington, was a butler for a well-known Washington physician and he sometimes worked as a caterer at the White House. Ellington said this about his father: "He raised his family as if he were a millionaire." His mother, Daisy, was the daughter of a police captain.

Ellington's older sibling died as a baby, so his mother took very special care of him. "I
25 was pampered and spoiled rotten by all the women in the family. My feet were not allowed to touch the ground until I was six." For example, when he got sick with pneumonia, his mother had two doctors see him. She also played the piano for him. When he was old enough to reach the piano keys, she gave him piano lessons, and like all mothers she made sure he practiced. Ellington said his mother made him feel like a
30 "very, very special child." In fact, he said, "My mother would say, 'Edward, you are blessed!' "

She also understood that life was hard. She believed that her son should feel that he "could do anything anyone else could do." She taught him to ignore racism. He grew up in a household that was full of love, where people did not talk about hostile incidents in the outside world.

A high school friend nicknamed Edward "Duke," and the nickname stuck. At the age of twelve, he started going to the theater and to clubs. He loved hearing the stories of people who had been to other cities such as Chicago and Cleveland. His ability to listen was one of his gifts.

Ellington was a talented painter and won a scholarship to study art at the Pratt Institute in New York. His interest in music was greater than his interest in art, though, so he pursued music as a career. At 17, he had a five-piece combo called the Washingtonians. He moved to New York in the early '20s and by 1926, he had an orchestra. The musicians in that orchestra stayed a long time. One player, Harry Carney, began in 1926 and stayed until he died in 1974. Because so many musicians stayed with the orchestra, they worked very well together.

Later Ellington's orchestra started playing at the Cotton Club in Harlem, an African American neighborhood in New York City. Playing at the Cotton Club made the orchestra famous. The Cotton Club was the place where wealthy whites went to hear what was called "jungle style" music. Ellington's orchestra played at the Cotton Club from 1927 to 1932.

Ellington's music was always considered ahead of its time and he was the first person to play longer pieces. At a time when pieces on records were usually three minutes long, Duke recorded "Creole Rhapsody," which was six and one-half minutes long.

Ellington wrote over 1,000 pieces. He composed music for the stage and for movies such as *Anatomy of a Murder* and *Paris Blues*. Some of his most famous compositions are "Sophisticated Lady," "Do Nothing Till You Hear From Me," and "I Got It Bad."

Word Count: 801

Source: *Jazz: A History of America's Music* (Ward and Burns)

Duke Ellington

Timed Reading

Read "A Jazz Great—Duke Ellington" again. Read at a comfortable speed. Time your reading.

Start time: _____

End time: _____

My reading time: _____

After You Read

Comprehension

A. Fill in the bubble of the sentence that best describes the main idea of "A Jazz Great—Duke Ellington."

- (A) Duke Ellington was a jazz great because he composed music for the stage and for movies.
- (B) Duke Ellington was a jazz great because he could mold a group of individual musicians.
- (C) Duke Ellington was a jazz great because he both played the piano and led the band.

B. Fill in the bubble for each correct answer.

1. When Duke Ellington says, "My thing is having fun," he means, "My main ____ is having fun."

- (A) difficulty
- (B) challenge
- (C) interest

2. When he said, "Ellington was a man who was an orchestra," Nat Hentoff meant ____.

- (A) Ellington could make one instrument sound like an orchestra
- (B) Ellington had so much talent he was like a whole orchestra
- (C) Ellington needed a whole orchestra to be successful

3. According to the article, Ellington combined Western European musical traditions with ____ tradition.

- (A) African oral
- (B) Western European oral
- (C) his own

4. According to the article, Duke Ellington ____.

- (A) received special care from his mother
- (B) had no sisters or brothers
- (C) had conflicts with his parents

5. Ellington gave up painting because he wanted to ____.

- (A) move to N.Y.
- (B) win a scholarship
- (C) pursue music

Talk About It

Discuss the following question with a partner. How were you treated as a child? Were you pampered and spoiled rotten? If so, in what ways? If not, explain why not.

How were you treated as a child?

I . . .

Reading 2: About Jazz

Before You Read

Preview

A. The title of Reading 2 is "About Jazz." What kind of information might it include? Discuss your ideas with a partner.

B. Preview these words from the reading. Complete each of the sentences below with the correct word.

> bucks   ensemble   entrepreneur   merges
> solo   subsidize   rural   urban

1. Charlie Parker lived in a(n) _____ area, the center of New York City.

2. Paul made a thousand _____ at his first concert. A thousand dollars is a lot of money for a first concert.

3. Sometimes cities _____ summer concerts. The city pays the musicians to play so that people can enjoy the music for free.

4. Mike was a(n) _____. He liked to start new businesses and he enjoyed both the risk and the responsibility of managing them.

5. Working together as a(n) _____, Robert and his group played lively jazz music.

6. Modern art _____ many different cultures. It brings together styles from different places and times to make something new.

7. As a(n) _____ piano player, Duke Ellington was great, but he didn't like to play alone as much as he liked to play with other musicians.

8. Many great blues singers grew up in _____ areas. They left the country farm or small town where they grew up to sing to large audiences in big cities.

Reading Skills

Using Topic Sentences to Preview a Reading

In previous chapters, you used titles, headings, pictures, captions, and introductions to preview a reading. Another way to preview is to read topic sentences. Topic sentences tell you what the body (middle) paragraphs of a reading are about. Body paragraphs usually include supporting ideas and specific details. They support and explain the main idea of the entire reading. So when you read the topic sentences, you can get a pretty good idea of how the author will support and explain his or her ideas. (**Note:** Topic sentences are often—but not always—the first sentence in each paragraph.)

Look at the first sentence from paragraph 2 of "The Geology of Mars" on page 151:

> Taking a look at the surface of Mars, we can see an enormous canyon, the Valles Marineris, that runs along the equator.

What can you expect to read about in this paragraph? → a description of a canyon on Mars.

Practice

A. Preview "About Jazz" on pages 197–199. Read and underline the first sentence of paragraphs 2–10.

B. Now write what you think each paragraph is about. Compare your answers with a partner.

Paragraph 2: _____

Paragraph 3: _____

Paragraph 4: _____

Paragraph 5: _____

Paragraph 6: _____

Paragraph 7: _____

Paragraph 8: _____

Paragraph 9: _____

Paragraph 10: _____

As You Read

As you read, think about this question:

► What cultures and musical styles influenced jazz?

Duke Ellington and his band in 1934

About Jazz

Duke Ellington defined jazz as "an American idiom with African roots." In fact, jazz—like American society and many societies around the world—is the product of many cultures and influences. In some ways, it merges cultures and musical styles; in other ways, it maintains ethnic characteristics.

5   Jazz began in the bars and nightclubs of poor urban neighborhoods. The first jazz performance was in the 1890s in New Orleans where Buddy Bolden led a jazz ensemble. Jazz styles—from traditional to swing to bebop—have changed over the years.

Today, all styles of jazz are studied in music schools and listened to all over the

10 world. Jazz has a strong following in continental Europe, Scandinavia, Japan, Africa, South America, and Canada. There are jazz festivals around the world every year. According to jazz festival entrepreneur George Wein, "There are probably 200 jazz festivals now. It's a reaction against rock—jazz is a good word and cities will give money to subsidize jazz festivals. They won't subsidize rock fes-

15 tivals. But just mention jazz and there's money there. Maybe not a lot—maybe just 10,000 bucks for concerts, maybe 30,000. But whatever it is, there's money there."

The roots of jazz are in the music that was played and listened to before its birth: popular songs, blues songs, ragtime, brass band numbers, and gospel music. In the late 19th and early 20th centuries, Americans—both African American and white—enjoyed these musical styles.

Popular songs then were those songs with great rhythms that were written and played in major keys. People often danced to them. Blues songs were written and played in a minor key. They are part of the oral tradition of folk music. They expressed the feelings of the oppressed African Americans in the Deep South and came from the work songs of slaves. They were originally sung by African American men who played the guitar as they sang. At the beginning of the 20th century, people in the cities started singing the blues, too.

By the 1920s, blues and jazz were tied together and frequently influenced each other. The most famous early jazz-blues singers were women such as Ma Rainey and Bessie Smith.

Ragtime also contributed to jazz. It has a regular pattern of march-like rhythm. The beat, which is normally weak, is stressed, or syncopated in ragtime. It originally was a form of popular music using a solo piano. It developed around St. Louis and its most popular writer and performer was Scott Joplin (1868–1917).

Ragtime traveled to New Orleans and other southern cities and was then arranged for instruments derived from popular African American brass bands.

Brass band music in New Orleans and other southern cities was played in many places. It was played in private African American clubs, social clubs, and fraternal organizations that employed African American musicians to play for dances, parties, parades, and funerals. A typical brass band had clarinets, trombones, cornets, banjos, bass horns, and drums. The first jazz pieces were arranged for similar instrumentation, but with only one player for each part.

Gospel music was happy-sounding, rhythmic, religious music. Early gospel music, particularly that of rural and illiterate African Americans, combined the sounds of the blues with exciting rhythms, high energy, and religious excitement.

> I lived a life but nothing I've gained
> Each day I'm full of sorrow and pain
> No one seems enough for poor me
> To give me a word of sympathy
> Oh me, oh my
> Wonder what will the end be
> Oh me, oh my
> Wonder what will become of poor me
> No father to guide, no mother to care
> Must bear my troubles all alone
> Not even a brother to help me share
> This burden I must bear alone
> Oh me, oh my
> Wonder what will the end be
> —*Bessie Smith, "Worried Life Blues"*

Blind Boys of Alabama

It is still popular today with both African Americans and whites.

The African Americans of the Deep South were of African heritage and usually had little opportunity for formal education. Whites and non-whites were educated according to western European traditions. The mixing of people from these two very different heritages—African and European—was the factor that, more than any other made, jazz grow and develop into a unique art. Interestingly, jazz is considered an art in a way that other music such as country, rock, or blues isn't.

Wynton Marsalis

Today many of the great players, sometimes called "The Young Lions," have been trained at music schools, such as the famous Berklee College of Music in Boston, Massachusetts. These musicians—Wynton Marsalis, Terence Blanchard, Nicholas Payton, Jon Faddis, Wallace Roney, Joshua Redman and James Carter—know both the theory and the history of jazz. This knowledge can be heard in their playing. Jazz critics point out how they are influenced by the jazz greats who came before them: Herbie Hancock, Louis Armstrong, Dizzy Gillespie, John Coltrane, Thelonious Monk, and Duke Ellington.

How will jazz change in the future? No one knows, but as Geoffrey Ward and Ken Burns report in their book, *Jazz: A History of America's Music*, "The writer Gary Giddins once asked the pianist Cedar Walton where he thought the music was going. 'It'll go wherever we take it' was the answer. 'We're the musicians.'"

Word Count: 785

Source: *Jazz: The World of Music* (Willoughby)

Timed Reading

Read "About Jazz" again. Read at a comfortable speed. Time your reading.

Start time: _____

End time: _____

My reading time: _____

After You Read

Main Idea

Which sentence best describes the main idea of "About Jazz"? Fill in the bubble of the correct answer.

(A) Jazz merges many traditions and cultures.

(B) Jazz has changed over the years.

(C) Jazz is studied in music schools around the world.

Reading Skills

Outlining

In Chapter 6, you learned about taking notes as you read. One way to take notes is to use an outline. Making an outline helps you find and remember the main ideas and details in a reading passage. It also helps you organize the ideas so you can easily review them later. A traditional outline has the following format:

Title

Introduction: Main Idea

I.   Supporting Idea # 1
    A. Specific Detail #1
    B. Specific Detail #2

II. Supporting Idea # 2
    A. Specific Detail #1
    B. Specific Detail #2

III. Supporting Idea #3
    A. Specific Detail #1
    B. Specific Detail #2
    Conclusion

Of course, a reading may have more, or fewer, than three supporting ideas. Look at the example on the next page. It's an outline of "Weather-Related Emergencies" in Chapter 8 on pages 168 and 169.

Title: *Weather-Related Emergencies*

Introduction: *It's important to know what to do in bad weather.*

I.   Supporting Idea # 1 *Lightning*
     A. Specific Detail #1 *Outdoors: stay low, avoid trees, metal*
     B. Specific Detail #2 *In a car: keep windows rolled up*
     C. Specific Detail #3 *Inside: don't touch anything in contact with outside*

II. Supporting Idea #2 *Floods*
     A. Specific Detail #1 *With lightning greatest cause of weather death and injury*
     B. Specific Detail #2 *Outside: get inside, or go to high place*
     C. Specific Detail #3 *In a car: go to a high place*
     D. Specific Detail #4 *Inside: watch out for animals*

III. Supporting Idea #3 *Sandstorms*
     A. Specific Detail #1 *Originate in China and Mongolia; go to Korea and Japan*
     B. Specific Detail #2 *Outside: wet cloth over nose and mouth, petroleum jelly, link arms, stay with group*
     C. Specific Detail #3 *In a car: get off road. Turn off lights.*
     D. Specific Detail #4 *Inside: stay until storm is over.*

Conclusion: *It's important to be prepared for weather emergencies. Radio, TV, and the safety section of the telephone book can help.*

Practice

A. Go back to the reading "About Jazz" and look over it again. On a separate piece of paper list each of the supporting ideas.

B. Now reread the passage and outline it on a separate piece of paper. Include the main idea, the supporting ideas, and specific details. Share your outline with a partner. Are they alike?

Getting the Details

A. Use your outline to answer the following questions regarding "About Jazz."

1. What five kinds of music influenced jazz? _____

    _____

2. What is one difference between popular songs and blues songs? _____

    _____

3. When did people in cities start singing the blues? _____

    _____

4. What was the most important factor in jazz developing into a unique art?

    _____

Vocabulary

A. Here are some more words and expressions from "About Jazz." Find them in the reading and circle them.

Nouns	Verb	Adjectives
festivals	derived from	illiterate
heritages		oppressed

B. Now use some of them to complete the sentences.

1. Jamie was _____ until the age of nine. Then she learned how to read and write.

2. African and European _____ were the traditions that combined to make jazz grow into the unique art it is today.

3. Ross is an entrepreneur who has organized many jazz _____, rock concerts, and other musical events. These organized series of performances have been very successful.

4. Improvisation in jazz is _____ _____ oral tradition.

5. In the 1920s African Americans were _____ and didn't have a lot of freedom.

Expressions

Time Expressions

In English, time expressions are a combination of a preposition and written or numerical numbers.

at + **age**   *by* + **specific time**   *in* + **period of time**

by + **period of time**   *from* (**time**) *to* (**time**)   *on* + **specific date**

Example:
Ellington's orghestra played at the Cotton Club from 1927 to 1932.

Practice

A. Find and underline the time expressions in the box in "A Jazz Great—Duke Ellington" or "About Jazz."

B. Then use the correct preposition in the following box with the correct time expression in the sentences below. (Note: You can use some prepositions more than once.)

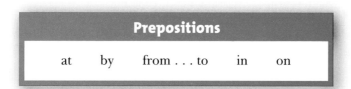

Prepositions				
at	by	from . . . to	in	on

1. Jazz great Miles Davis was born _____ May 26, 1926, in Alton, Illinois.

2. Davis began playing the trumpet _____ the age of 13.

3. _____ 1946 _____ 1947, Davis was a regular member of the Billy Eckstine band.

4. _____ the mid-1950s, Davis organized his first quintet (group of five musicians).

5. _____ the late 1960s, Davis started using electronic instruments in his music.

6. In the late 1970s, Davis stopped performing, but _____ the early 1980s, he started playing again.

Internet Research

Using a Music Dictionary

There are many specialized dictionaries on the Internet. Specialized dictionaries help you understand vocabulary in a particular area. Music dictionaries are one kind of specialized dictionary. To find a word related to jazz online, go to a music dictionary such as the Virginia Tech Multimedia Music Dictionary (www.music.vt.edu/musicdictionary/) or a jazz dictionary site like NewToJazz.com (www.newtojazz.com/dictionary.asp?section=dictionary).

For most online dictionaries, you should start by choosing the letter of the term that you want to look up.

Example: Click on *s* to find a definition of *syncopation*.

a b c d e f g h i j k l m n o p q r s t u v w x y z

Practice

Look up the following words and write the definitions on the lines below. Use an online music or jazz dictionary such as newtojazz.com, or do a search for "jazz dictionary." Then tell the class whether or not you found the words, how you found them, and what they mean.

1. bebop _____

2. big band _____

3. boogie-woogie _____

4. ensemble _____

5. jazz _____

6. jazz band _____

7. smooth jazz _____

8. swing _____

Write About It

A. Write the following paragraphs. Fill in the blanks. Write complete sentences.

Paragraph One

I like _____ music for two reasons. One reason
(Give a type of music you like)

I like it is that _____. For
(Give one reason why you like it)

example, _____.
(Give an example of this reason from a song or other piece of music)

Another reason I like it is that _____

_____.
(Give another reason why you like it)

For example, _____.
(Give an example of this reason from a song or other piece of music)

Paragraph Two

Jazz music is a unique combination of many kinds of music. One type of music that has

influenced jazz is _____.
(Give one type of music that has influenced jazz)

This type of music _____

_____.
(Describe this type of music)

Another type of music is _____.
(Give another type of music that has influenced jazz)

This type of music _____

_____.
(Describe this type of music)

B. Now write your own paragraphs. Write one paragraph about your favorite type of music and another about influences on jazz. Try to include words and expressions from this chapter and your Internet research in your paragraphs.

C. Write more paragraphs about music. Use five words and expressions from this chapter and your Internet research. Choose from the following topics.

▶ Write about your favorite musician or composer.

▶ Describe when and where you like to listen to music.

▶ Describe a concert or music festival that you attended.

▶ If you play a musical instrument, describe how you learned to play it.

▶ What instrument would you like to play? Explain why.

▶ Use your own idea.

Charlie Parker

On Your Own

Project

Give a presentation about your favorite song. Make a summary chart of favorite songs for the whole class.

Step 1: Practice

Listen to your favorite song. Take notes on why you like it. Do Internet research, if necessary, for musical terms that you can use in your presentation.

Practice your presentation. Have your teacher listen to make sure you are pronouncing words correctly.

Step 2: Give a Presentation

Bring a tape or CD of your favorite song to class. Play it for the class and explain why it's your favorite. Make eye contact with your audience.

After all the presentations, make a summary chart of the class's favorite songs. Use the following chart or a similar one. (Be careful, some people don't like to give their age. If someone says, "I'd rather not say," just put a range (e.g., 20-30) in the space for age. Ask only once.)

Favorite Songs				
Student's Name	Age	Favorite Song	Type of Song	Reason for Liking It

Step 3: Follow-Up

Discuss the chart. What are the top three kinds of music? Do any students share the same favorite song? Is there any kind of music that only one or two people say is their favorite? Is there any relationship between the age of a person and the kind of music he or she likes?

Wrap Up

How Much Do You Remember?

Check your new knowledge. In this chapter you learned facts, words, and expressions. You also learned reading skills and you practiced writing. Complete the following to check what you remember.

1. Why is Duke Ellington a jazz great? _____

_____

2. What types of music influenced jazz? _____

_____

3. What does *improvisation* mean? _____

4. Use the expression *derived from* in a sentence. _____

_____

5. How can reading the first sentence of each paragraph in a passage help you preview it?

_____

_____

6. What is the purpose of making an outline as you read? _____

_____

7. How can you find the definition of a word such as *syncopation* on the Internet? _____

_____

Second Timed Readings

Now reread "A Jazz Great—Duke Ellington" and "About Jazz." Time each reading separately. Write your times in the Timed Reading Chart on page 238.

Crossword Puzzle

Complete the crossword puzzle to practice some words from this chapter.

CLUES

Across →
1. Alone
7. In the country
8. An informal word for "money"
9. Traditions
10. A group of musicians

Down ↓
2. Not given freedom or rights
3. Cannot read or write
4. In the city
5. Very well taken care of
6. Support with money

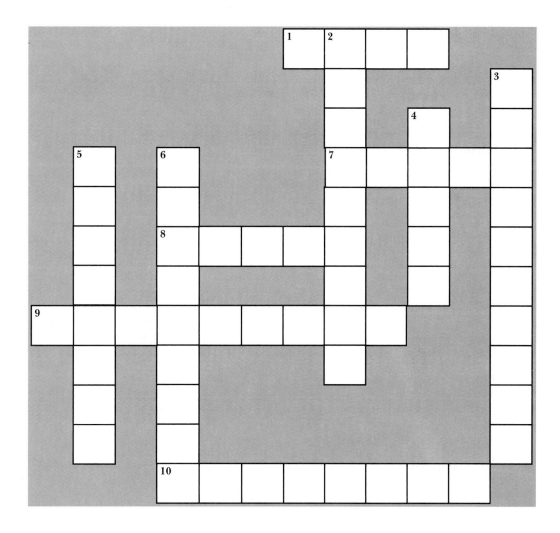

10 Art History: Asian Influences on Western Art

CHAPTER PREVIEW

In this chapter, you'll:

Content
► read a website about the art collection at the Freer and Sackler galleries in Washington, DC
► learn how Asian art influenced Western art in the 19th century

Reading Skills
► combine several strategies to preview a reading
► summarize the main ideas of a reading

Vocabulary Skills
► use words and expressions to talk about art and artists
► use expressions to discuss artistic influences

Writing Skills
► describe your favorite work of art
► explain the influences in a work of art

Internet Skills
► use the "Find" feature to locate specific information on a web page

I don't know anything about art, but I know what I like. 🐌

—*Gelett Burgess*
(American humorist, 1866–1951)

SHORT SURVEY

My favorite kind of art is:

❑ photography

❑ painting

❑ sculpture

❑ drawing

❑ other _____

Reading 1:

What kind of art can you see at the Freer and Sackler galleries in Washington, DC? Read "Current Exhibitions: The Freer and Sackler Galleries" to find out.

Reading 2:

How did Asian art influence European and American art? "Crossing Cultures: *Japonisme* and Western Art" has some answers.

What do you think?

Answer the questions about art and you. Then ask your partner about his or her experiences with art. Discuss your answers.

What kind of art do you like to create?

I . . .

Art and You

1. I like to create art. Yes No

   If yes, what type of art do you like to create (photography, painting, drawing, etc.)?

   _____

2. I like to look at art. Yes No

   If yes, what type of art do you like to look at? _____

3. I like to go to museums and galleries*. Yes No

4. The last time I went to a museum was (time) _____

   and I saw (type of art) _____.

5. I like to look at art on museum websites. Yes No

   If yes, what are your favorite museum websites? _____

6. I like to study art history. Yes No

7. I like to read about art. Yes No

8. I like to read about artists' lives. Yes No

9. My favorite work of art is _____.

   Or: ___ I don't have a favorite work of art.

10. My favorite artist is _____.

    Or: ___ I don't have a favorite artist.

*Small museums

Reading 1: Current Exhibitions: The Freer and Sackler Galleries

Before You Read

Preview

A. The title of Reading 1 is "Current Exhibitions: The Freer and Sackler Galleries." It's a museum website. What kind of information might it include? Discuss your ideas with a partner.

B. Do you know these types of art and art objects? Take the quiz. Match each type of art with its correct description. Write the letter of the correct description on the line.

Types of Art and Art Objects

_____ **1.** calligraphy

_____ **3.** porcelain

_____ **2.** ceramics

_____ **4.** sculpture

Descriptions

a. a three-dimensional object that is modeled (for example, from clay), carved (for example, from wood), or put together (for example, from pieces of metal)

b. the art of making objects of clay and firing (heating) them in a special oven called a *kiln*

c. clay mixed with other minerals and fired (heated) at extremely high temperatures, much higher than those for ceramics; often used for dinnerware, vases, and smaller sculptures

d. artistic handwriting using quills (feathers), brushes, or pens with ink

Vocabulary

Here are some words and expressions from "Current Exhibitions: The Freer and Sackler Galleries." Match each word or expression with its correct meaning. Write the letter of the answer on the line.

Words and Expressions

_____ 1. art for art's sake

_____ 2. bronze

_____ 3. caliphs

_____ 4. exhibition

_____ 5. luxury

_____ 6. melting pot

_____ 7. pottery

_____ 8. vessels

Meanings

a. containers

b. an idea about art: art for enjoyment instead of art for teaching a lesson

c. not a necessity

d. a mixing of cultures

e. objects made from clay

f. a hard, yellow metal sometimes used to make pots and containers

g. a title used in the past for an Islamic ruler

h. a showing of art

Visitors at the Art Institute in Chicago, Illinois

As You Read

You are going to read a webpage for the Freer and Sackler Galleries of Art in Washington, DC. It contains information about exhibitions at the museum. As you read, think about this question: What types of art and art objects can you see at the Freer and Sackler galleries?

All art is an individual's expression of a culture. Cultures differ, so art looks different. ॐ

—Henry Glassie (American professor of folklore, b.1941)

Current Exhibitions: The Freer and Sackler Galleries

exhibitions

VISITOR INFORMATION | EXHIBITIONS | EVENTS | THE COLLECTIONS | EDUCATION

search site

PAST EXHIBITIONS
CURRENT EXHIBITIONS
FUTURE EXHIBITIONS
ONLINE EXHIBITIONS

S M T W T F S

CALENDAR

Return of the Buddha   Caliphs & Kings   Whistler in Paris

FEATURED EXHIBITIONS

Faith and Form: Selected Calligraphy and Painting from Japanese Religious Traditions
Through July 18, 2004

Return of the Buddha: The Qingzhou Discoveries
Through August 8, 2004

Whistler in Paris: Lithographs from the Belle Epoque, 1891-1896
Through August 15, 2004

Perspectives: Do-Ho Suh
Through September 26, 2004

Caliphs and Kings: The Art and Influence of Islamic Spain
Through October 17, 2004

COMPLETE LIST OF EXHIBITIONS

AMERICAN ART

Whistler in Paris: Lithographs from the Belle Epoque, 1891-1896
The Peacock Room
James McNeill Whistler (1834-1903)
Art for Art's Sake

RELATED TOPICS

TOURS, TALKS & LECTURES
Learn more about exhibition-related events

IMAGINASIA FAMILY PROGRAMS
Learn more about events for young visitors

SUPPORT US
Your generosity helps support our exhibitions. Click here to find out how.

BUDDHA

BUY ASIAN ART BOOKS ONLINE
Return of the Buddha: The Qingzhou Discoveries

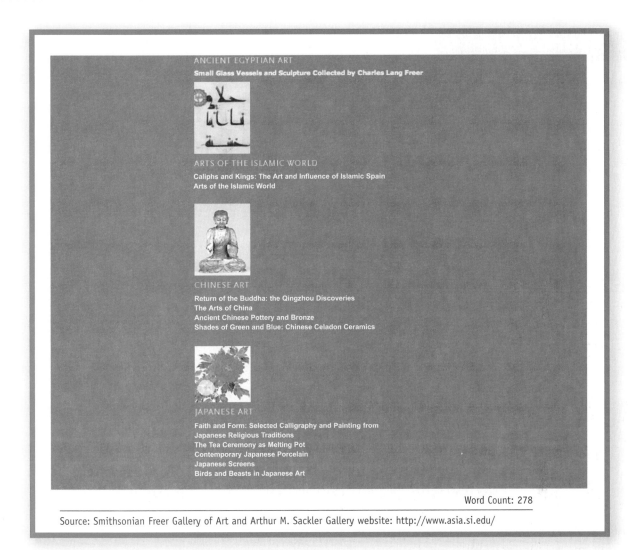

ANCIENT EGYPTIAN ART

Small Glass Vessels and Sculpture Collected by Charles Lang Freer

ARTS OF THE ISLAMIC WORLD

Caliphs and Kings: The Art and Influence of Islamic Spain
Arts of the Islamic World

CHINESE ART

Return of the Buddha: the Qingzhou Discoveries
The Arts of China
Ancient Chinese Pottery and Bronze
Shades of Green and Blue: Chinese Celadon Ceramics

JAPANESE ART

Faith and Form: Selected Calligraphy and Painting from Japanese Religious Traditions
The Tea Ceremony as Melting Pot
Contemporary Japanese Porcelain
Japanese Screens
Birds and Beasts in Japanese Art

Word Count: 278

Source: Smithsonian Freer Gallery of Art and Arthur M. Sackler Gallery website: http://www.asia.si.edu/

Timed Reading

Read "Current Exhibitions: Freer and Sackler Galleries" again. Read at a comfortable speed. Time your reading.

Start time: _____

End time: _____

My reading time: _____

After You Read

Comprehension

A. Fill in the bubble that best completes the main idea of "Current Exhibitions: The Freer and Sackler Galleries."

At the Freer and Sackler Galleries, you can see mostly _____ art.

    (A) American   (B) Japanese   (C) Asian

B. Fill in the bubble for each correct answer.

1. At the Freer and Sackler galleries, you can see lithographs from _____.

    (A) Paris   (B) Japan   (C) China

2. At the Freer and Sackler galleries, you can see ceramics from _____.

    (A) Japan   (B) China   (C) Korea

3. What is *Return of the Buddha: The Qingzhou Discoveries*?

    (A) a painting title   (B) an exhibition title   (C) both A and B

4. What color are *celadon* ceramics from China?

    (A) gold and blue   (B) red and blue   (C) green and blue

5. James McNeill Whistler is probably _____.

    (A) a French artist   (B) an American artist   (C) a Japanese artist

Talk About It

Discuss the following questions with a partner.

1. Why do you think that the Freer and Sackler galleries show the art of an American (James McNeill Whistler)? What type of art might it be?

2. Name an artist from your culture or country. What type of art does he or she create?

Why do you think . . .

I think . . .

Reading 2: Crossing Cultures: *Japonisme* and Western Art

Before You Read

Preview

The title of Reading 2 is "Crossing Cultures: *Japonisme* and Western Art." You read about "crossing cultures" in Chapter 3. What might this phrase mean when people are talking about art? What do you think *Japonisme* means? What country name does it remind you of? What might be some differences between Western art and other types of art? Discuss your ideas with a partner.

Reading Skills

> ### Review: Putting It All Together
>
> In previous chapters, you used titles, headings, pictures and captions, introductions and conclusions, and topic sentences to preview a reading passage. Together, these strategies are powerful previewing tools. Now it's time to put them all together.

Practice

Answer these questions about "Crossing Cultures: *Japonisme* and Western Art" on pages 220–223.

1. **Title:** Review your answers to the Preview exercise above. What ideas do you have about the passage from reading the title?

   _____

2. **Headings:** Read the first heading on page 220. What do you think this section is about?

   _____

   Read the second heading on page 220. What do you think this section is about? _____

   _____

   Read the third heading on page 221. What do you think this section is about? _____

   _____

3. **Topic Sentences:** Find and read the topic sentences. What are the following paragraphs about?

Paragraph 2: _____

Paragraph 3: _____

Paragraph 4: _____

Paragraph 5: _____

Paragraph 6: _____

Paragraph 7: _____

4. **Pictures:** Look at the pictures. Read their captions. What information do they give you about

the passage? _____

5. Now answer this question: What is "Crossing Cultures: *Japonisme* and Western Art" probably about?

  (A) the influence of one type of Western art on Japanese art and artists

  (B) the influence of one type of Japanese art on Western art and artists

  (C) the influence of one Japanese artist on Western art and artists

> The painting has a life of its own. I try to let it come through. ❧
>
> —*Jackson Pollock (American painter, 1912–1956)*

Preview these words from the reading. Match each word with its correct meaning. Write the letter of the correct meaning on the line.

Words	Meanings
_____ **1.** carving	**a.** showed
_____ **2.** controversial	**b.** obvious; easy to see
_____ **3.** distinctive	**c.** actions of a group of people
_____ **4.** evident	**d.** objects covered with thick, shiny paint
_____ **5.** exemplifies	**e.** noticeable because it's different or unique
_____ **6.** lacquerware	**f.** cutting with a knife
_____ **7.** movements	**g.** something about which people don't agree
_____ **8.** represented	**h.** is an example of

Here are some words used to discuss paintings. With a partner, read the words and definitions. Then find an example of each word in the picture below.

The Scream, *Edvard Munch*

1. **foreground**—the part of a painting that is nearest to and in front of the viewer
2. **background**—the part of a painting representing what lies behind objects in the foreground
3. **composition**—the combination and placement of different objects within a painting
4. **perspective**—the representation of three-dimensional objects on a flat surface to create the impression of distance and relative size

As you read, think about this question:

▶ Which characteristics of Japanese art can you see in some famous European and American paintings?

🎧 Crossing Cultures: *Japonisme* and Western Art

Nocturne in Blue and Gold
(Old Battersea Bridge), *James Whistler*

Riverside Bamboo Market,
Kyobashi, *Ando Hiroshige*

Cross-cultural artistic exchange between the West and the East goes back to the time of early civilization. Starting around 2300 B.C., Mesopotamia exchanged goods and art ideas with India. Chinese lacquerware and other goods found their way to Rome during the Roman empire, and European explorers discovered Japanese
5   artists during the Renaissance. However, one of the most active periods in Western art, the 19th century, owes much to the influence of Japanese art.

Japonisme

One well-known 19th century artist, the American James Abbott McNeill Whistler, was controversial in his day because his work didn't conform to traditional artistic standards. In fact, the English art critic John Ruskin accused Whistler of "flinging a
10   pot of paint in the public's face." However, much of Whistler's work, especially *Nocturne in Blue and Gold (Old Battersea Bridge)*, actually exemplifies *Japonisme*. *Japonisme* refers to the 19th century influence of Japanese art and culture on Western art movements such as Impressionism, Art Nouveau, and Symbolism.

Japanese Woodblock Prints

In the 19th century, Japan, after being closed for over two hundred years, suddenly
15   was open for foreigners to visit. This change allowed increased contact with the United States and Europe. Americans, Europeans, and the British became interested

in anything Japanese. European artists were particularly influenced by Japanese woodblock prints that were imported to Europe at that time.

Japanese woodblock prints became popular in Japan during the Edo period (1603–1868). Called *ukiyo-e* ("pictures of the floating world"), these prints showed the pleasures of everyday life in the city and the beauty of nature. It was a new form of art, available for everyone to enjoy. Important artists of this style were Ando Hiroshige, Katsushika Hokusai, and Kitagawa Utamaro. Woodblock prints were made by carving a design into a piece of wood, painting the wood, and then pressing the wood onto paper to make the print.

In terms of color and composition, *ukiyo-e* prints have certain characteristics. The colors are usually bold and bright. The composition is particularly distinctive because forms in the prints are flat and without shading. There is often a diagonal line that moves from the bottom right to the top left of the picture, forcing the eye to move to the background. This acts as a kind of perspective device. The diagonal line is clearly evident in Hiroshige's *Fireworks at Ryogoku*. Also, there is often a cut-off object in the picture, such as a lamppost or pillar; the viewer sees only part of it in the foreground, and it blocks part of the view. An example of this is the bridge in Hiroshige's *Riverside Bamboo Market, Kyobashi*. This gives the viewer the feeling of being in the picture, not just observing it from the outside.

Fireworks at Ryogoku,
Ando Hiroshige

The Influence of Japanese Prints on Western Art

Japanese prints were the subject of a major Paris exhibition in 1890, and they made a deep impression on painters living and working in France at the time. Many of these artists borrowed not only colors and compositional elements from Japanese prints, but also often the subject matter. You can see their influence in the works of Mary Cassatt, Edgar Degas, Toulouse-Lautrec, and of course, James McNeill Whistler.

Mary Cassatt, an American artist living in Paris, was particularly influenced by Kitagawa Utamaro, whose works were shown at the 1890 exhibit. Utamaro specialized in images of beautiful women in everyday settings. His influence on Cassatt is noticeable in many of her paintings, including *The Letter* (page 222). The subject matter of *The Letter* is similar to that of Utamaro: an attractive woman in an everyday activity. In addition, the choice of colors in *The Letter*—bold blues—and the flat, unshaded forms are directly influenced by Japanese woodblock prints.

The Letter,
Mary Cassatt

Woman Reading a Letter,
Kitagawa Utamaro

Two other artists who were influenced by Japanese prints include Edgar Degas and Toulouse-Lautrec. Degas borrowed the *ukiyo-e* compositional device of a cut-off object in the foreground in *Women at a Café, Evening* (1877). In this painting, posts block the view of the café scene. For Henri de Toulouse-Lautrec, his signature flat,

55 unshaded forms and bright, bold colors in works such as *Moulin-Rouge La Goulue* (1891) were influenced by the style of the Japanese print. The American artist Whistler not only used color and compositional elements from Japanese prints in his works, but also Japanese objects, designs, and symbols. An example is Whistler's *The Princess from the Land of Porcelain* (1863–64), a full-length portrait of a woman in a

60 kimono standing in front of a Japanese screen.

The influence of Japanese woodblock prints is present in the work of many other European artists, such as Gustave Klimt (Austrian), Vincent Van Gogh (Dutch), Claude Monet (French), Paul Gauguin (French), and Paul Cezanne (French). This 19th century cross-cultural exchange of artistic concepts changed the way that many

65 Western artists viewed and represented the world.

Word Count: 800

Source: *Gilbert's Living with Art* (Getlein)

Timed Reading

Read "Crossing Cultures: *Japonisme* and Western Art" again. Read at a comfortable speed. Time your reading.

Start time: _____

End time: _____

My reading time: _____

After You Read

Main Idea

Which sentence best describes the main idea of "Crossing Cultures: *Japonisme* and Western Art"? Fill in the bubble of the correct answer.

- Ⓐ Japanese art and culture influenced 19th-century Western art.
- Ⓑ Japanese art appeared in a major Paris exhibition in the 19th century.
- Ⓒ Japanese art and culture was unknown in 19th-century Europe.

Getting the Details

A. Fill in the bubble for each correct answer.

1. Which statement is true?

   - Ⓐ There was no cross-cultural exchange of art between the East and the West before the 19th century.
   - Ⓑ European explorers discovered Japanese art during the Renaissance.
   - Ⓒ There was no Asian art during the Roman empire.

2. What event allowed Westerners to learn about Japanese art?

   - Ⓐ In the 19th century, Japan started creating a new kind of art in the form of woodblock prints.
   - Ⓑ In the 19th century, the United States and Europe allowed Westerners to visit Japan.
   - Ⓒ In the 19th century, Japan was open to foreigners to visit for the first time in 200 years.

3. Which statement about *ukiyo-e* is true?

   - Ⓐ It usually has bold colors and no shading.
   - Ⓑ It always has a picture of a bridge in the foreground.
   - Ⓒ It always has a diagonal line from the bottom left to the top right.

4. Which Japanese artist's influence can be seen in *The Letter*?

   - Ⓐ Katsushika Hokusai
   - Ⓑ Kitagawa Utamaro
   - Ⓒ Ando Hiroshige

5. Which Western painting has a cut-off object in the foreground?

(A) *The Letter*

(B) *Women at a Café, Evening*

(C) *Riverside Bamboo Market, Kyobashi*

Reading Skills

Summarizing

In Chapter 5, you saw that paraphrasing—restating in your own words—an author's ideas can help you understand and remember them. Summarizing is a similar skill. Summarizing is writing a shorter version of an entire passage in your own words. Writing a summary is one way to take notes on and remember reading passages. Summaries help you study for tests and write papers.

A summary has certain characteristics:

▶ it is shorter than the original passage

▶ it tells only the main ideas

▶ it does not give a lot of detailed information or specific examples

▶ it does not give opinions about the passage

▶ it mentions the title and/or the author of the passage

Look at this summary of "The Geology of Mars" on pages 151–153 of Chapter 7 as an example:

"The Geology of Mars" describes the geological features of the surface and the atmosphere of Mars and compares them to those on Earth. Like Earth, Mars has polar ice caps, deserts, high mountains, clouds, and wind. Unlike Earth, there is very little water. Scientists, however, have found a great deal of evidence that there was water on Mars in the past. They're not sure what happened to the water, but they continue to study this because it may mean that there was once life on Mars.

To write a summary, follow these steps:

▶ Reread the passage.

▶ Take notes as you read. Put the main ideas in your own words.

▶ Reread what you wrote. Make sure you have only the main ideas. Make sure you don't include opinions.

▶ Revise if necessary.

Practice

Write a summary of "Crossing Cultures: *Japonisme* and Western Art." Compare your summary with a partner. Answer the following questions about your partner's summary.

1. How long is the summary?
2. Did your partner include all the main ideas?
3. Did your partner include *only* the main ideas?
4. Does the summary mention the title of the passage?
5. Is there any information that should not be in the summary? Is there any information that should be in the summary but is not?

Vocabulary

A. Here are some more words and expressions from "Crossing Cultures: *Japonisme* and Western Art." Find them in the reading and circle them.

Nouns	Verbs	Preposition
a. artistic standards b. signature	c. conform to d. found their way	e. in (his day)

B. Now match each one with an underlined word or expression in a sentence. Write the letter of the correct word or expression on the line.

_____ **1.** Toulouse-Lautrec's use of color was a <u>very identifiable characteristic</u> of his art.

_____ **2.** <u>During his lifetime</u>, Whistler was considered to be controversial.

_____ **3.** James McNeill Whistler had his own <u>ideas about how art should be</u>; he didn't try to please the art critics.

_____ **4.** Whistler was an individual; he didn't <u>follow</u> other artists' styles.

_____ **5.** Asian art objects <u>came</u> to Europe during the Roman Empire.

Discuss this question in small groups.

Look at this painting by Vincent van Gogh. What characteristics of *Japonisme* do you see?

The Sower, Vincent van Gogh

Expressions

Discussing Artistic Influences

You can use expressions with the word *influence* to talk about how cultures, artistic styles, or artists influence one another. There are other expressions that you can also use to discuss artistic influence.

Influence	Example:
influence of	
influence in (the work/s of)	I see an Asian influence in the work of
influence on (her)	Toulouse-Lautrec.
were influenced by	
Other Expressions	
owes much to	
made an impression on	Japanese woodblock prints made an
borrowed . . . from	impression on many European artists.

Practice

A. Find and underline the expressions from the box in "Current Exhibitions: The Freer and Sackler Galleries" or "Crossing Cultures: *Japonisme* and Western Art."

B. Now use some of them to complete the sentences about the following artistic facts. (Note: There may be more than one correct expression for the sentences.)

1. In Spain, you can see the _____ _____ Islamic art in the architecture of Spain.

2. The work of Toulouse-Lautrec _____ _____ _____ the art of Japan.

3. Many American and European artists _____ _____ _____ Japanese art and culture during the 19th century.

4. You can see Hiroshige's _____ _____ Whistler in his painting *Nocturne in Blue and Gold (Old Battersea Bridge)*.

5. The exhibition of Japanese art in Paris during the late 1800s _____

   _____ _____ _____ many French artists.

Internet Research

Finding Specific Information on a Webpage

You can find a specific word or phrase quickly on a webpage using the *Find* function of your browser. This is especially useful on pages that have a great deal of text. To do this, open a webpage. Use the Edit pull-down menu in your browser and select *Find*. In the Find textbox, write the word or phrase that you want to locate on the page. (Note: You don't need to use capital letters if it's a name.) Then click the *Find* button, and the first instance of the word or phrase on the page will be highlighted. To find the word or phrase again on the page, select "Find Again" from the Edit pull-down menu and the next instance will be highlighted.

Practice

Practice using the *Find* function to locate more examples of *Japonisme* on the Internet. Use a search engine (such as google.com) to do a search for "japonisme." Choose a webpage about *Japonisme* and use *Find* to locate on the page information on a particular artist or work of art. Collect information on one of the following artists from the box below, or try your own words and phrases.

Keywords		
Mary Cassatt	Katsushika Hokusai	KitagawaUtamro
Edgar Degas	Claude Monet	Vincent van Gogh
Paul Gauguin	Henri de Toulouse-Lautrec	
Ando Hiroshige	Ukiyo-e	

Share your *Find* experience and your results with your classmates.

Write About It

A. Write the following paragraphs. Fill in the blanks. Write complete sentences.

Paragraph One

My favorite work of art is _____ by _____.

(Give the title)   (Give the artist's name)

I like it because _____

(Give one reason why you like it)

_____.

For example, _____.

(Give an example that illustrates this reason)

It's also my favorite because _____

(Give another reason why you like it)

_____.

For example, _____.

(Give an example that illustrates this reason)

Paragraph Two

_____ by _____ is an example of

(Give the title of a work of art)   (Give the artist's name)

Japonisme. One characteristic of *Japonisme* that you can see in this picture is _____

_____. For example, _____

(Give a characteristic of *Japonisme*)   (Describe something that exemplifies the characteristic)

_____.

Another characteristic is _____. For example,

(Give another characteristic of *Japonisme*)

_____.

(Describe something that exemplifies this characteristic)

B. Now write your own paragraphs. Write one paragraph about a favorite work of art and another about an example of *Japonisme*. Try to include words and expressions from this chapter in your paragraphs.

C. Write more paragraphs about art, artists, and artistic influences. Use five words and expressions from this chapter and your Internet research. Choose from the following topics.

▶ Compare two works of art.

▶ Is it important to study art history? Why or why not?

▶ Would you like to be an artist? Why or why not?

▶ Can anyone create art? Why or why not?

▶ Describe the influences of a type of art or a culture on another work of art.

▶ Use your own idea.

Fireworks at Ryogoku, *Ando Hiroshige*

> **Great artists have no country.** ♨
>
> —*Alfred de Musset
> (French author, 1810–1857)*

On Your Own

Project

Give a presentation on a work of art or an artist. Do research with a partner.

Step 1: Practice

Collect facts about and pictures of your subject. If you choose a work of art, collect information on things that you can see in the picture such as the composition, the color, perspective, and any influences that it illustrates from other types of art. If you choose an artist, find facts about his or her life, examples of his or her work, and any influences on that work.

Write notes for your presentation. You can use the box below. Practice your presentation with your partner. Have your teacher listen to make sure you are pronouncing words correctly.

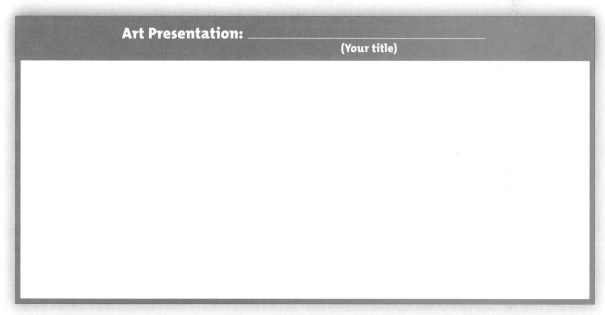

Art Presentation: _____
(Your title)

Step 2: Give a Presentation

Give your presentation to the class with your partner. Take turns speaking. Show your picture. Make eye contact with your audience. The audience should take notes and ask questions afterward.

Step 3: Follow-Up

Discuss your presentations. Which were interesting? What made them interesting? What did you like about your presentation? What will you do differently next time?

Wrap Up

How Much Do You Remember?

Check your new knowledge. In this chapter you learned facts, words, and expressions. You also learned reading skills and you practiced writing. Complete the following to check what you remember.

1. Name three types of art that you can see at the Freer and Sackler galleries. _____
   _____

2. Give three characteristics of Japanese woodblock prints. _____
   _____

3. How is a summary different from an original passage? _____
   _____

4. What is *porcelain*? _____

5. Use *background* and *foreground* in a sentence about *The Sower* on page 226. _____
   _____

6. Use *was/were influenced by* in a sentence. _____
   _____

7. How can you find a specific word or phrase on a webpage? _____
   _____

Second Timed Readings

Now reread "Current Exhibitions: The Freer and Sackler Galleries" and "Crossing Cultures: *Japonisme* and Western Art." Time each reading separately. Write your times in the Timed Reading Chart on page 238.

Crossword Puzzle

Complete the crossword puzzle to practice some words and expressions from this chapter.

CLUES

Across ➜

1. Objects made from clay
3. Showed
7. Artistic handwriting
8. Whistler didn't _____ _____ other people's ideas about art.

Down ⬇

2. Is an example of
4. A three-dimensional work of art
5. You can see the _____ _____ Japanese art in Whistler's paintings.
6. The part of the picture that is closest to the viewer
7. Cutting a design into something such as wood

Timed Reading Chart

Use this chart to keep track of your reading times.

CHAPTER 1: How to Read a Textbook

I Can't Believe How Much Reading We Have to Do!   **Page 8**

First Reading

Start time: _____

End time: _____

My reading time: _____

Second Reading

Start time: _____

End time: _____

My reading time: _____

Active Reading   **Page 14**

First Reading

Start time: _____

End time: _____

My reading time: _____

Second Reading

Start time: _____

End time: _____

My reading time: _____

CHAPTER 2: Test-Taking Skills

Types of Tests   **Page 30**

First Reading

Start time: _____

End time: _____

My reading time: _____

Second Reading

Start time: _____

End time: _____

My reading time: _____

How to Prepare for a Test   **Page 35**

First Reading

Start time: _____

End time: _____

My reading time: _____

Second Reading

Start time: _____

End time: _____

My reading time: _____

UNIT 2 History

CHAPTER 3: World History: 1000–1500 A.D.

Ibn Battuta: Long-Distance Traveler   Page 54
First Reading

Start time: _____

End time: _____

My reading time: _____

Second Reading

Start time: _____

End time: _____

My reading time: _____

Cross-Cultural Exchange: 1000–1500 A.D.   Page 59
First Reading

Start time: _____

End time: _____

My reading time: _____

Second Reading

Start time: _____

End time: _____

My reading time: _____

CHAPTER 4: The History of Flight

On Flight   Page 76
First Reading

Start time: _____

End time: _____

My reading time: _____

Second Reading

Start time: _____

End time: _____

My reading time: _____

Flight Firsts   Page 81
First Reading

Start time: _____

End time: _____

My reading time: _____

Second Reading

Start time: _____

End time: _____

My reading time: _____

Timed Reading Chart

Use this chart to keep track of your reading times.

U N I T 3 Business

CHAPTER 5: Jobs

Personality and Job Choice   **Page 100**
First Reading   **Second Reading**

Start time: _____   Start time: _____

End time: _____   End time: _____

My reading time: _____   My reading time: _____

What U.S. Employers Want   **Page 106**
First Reading   **Second Reading**

Start time: _____   Start time: _____

End time: _____   End time: _____

My reading time: _____   My reading time: _____

CHAPTER 6: International Marketing

An Interview with a Branding Consultant   **Page 122**
First Reading   **Second Reading**

Start time: _____   Start time: _____

End time: _____   End time: _____

My reading time: _____   My reading time: _____

International Marketing: Strategies for Success   **Page 127**
First Reading   **Second Reading**

Start time: _____   Start time: _____

End time: _____   End time: _____

My reading time: _____   My reading time: _____

CHAPTER 7: Mars

Mars and the Human Imagination   **Page 146**
First Reading   **Second Reading**

Start time: _____   Start time: _____

End time: _____   End time: _____

My reading time: _____   My reading time: _____

The Geology of Mars   **Page 151**
First Reading   **Second Reading**

Start time: _____   Start time: _____

End time: _____   End time: _____

My reading time: _____   My reading time: _____

CHAPTER 8: Meteorology

Weather-Related Emergencies   **Page 168**
First Reading   **Second Reading**

Start time: _____   Start time: _____

End time: _____   End time: _____

My reading time: _____   My reading time: _____

How Weather Prediction Works   **Page 173**
First Reading   **Second Reading**

Start time: _____   Start time: _____

End time: _____   End time: _____

My reading time: _____   My reading time: _____

Timed Reading Chart

Use this chart to keep track of your reading times.

UNIT 5 The Arts

CHAPTER 9: Jazz

A Jazz Great—Duke Ellington   **Page 192**

First Reading   **Second Reading**

Start time: _____   Start time: _____

End time: _____   End time: _____

My reading time: _____   My reading time: _____

About Jazz   **Page 197**

First Reading   **Second Reading**

Start time: _____   Start time: _____

End time: _____   End time: _____

My reading time: _____   My reading time: _____

CHAPTER 10: Art History: Asian Influences on Western Art

Current Exhibitions: The Freer and Sackler Galleries   **Page 214**

First Reading   **Second Reading**

Start time: _____   Start time: _____

End time: _____   End time: _____

My reading time: _____   My reading time: _____

Crossing Cultures: *Japonisme* and Western Art   **Page 220**

First Reading   **Second Reading**

Start time: _____   Start time: _____

End time: _____   End time: _____

My reading time: _____   My reading time: _____

Vocabulary Index

Chapter 1

analyze
auditory (type of learner)
come back to (something)
comprehend
concepts
demanding
enormous link
focus your attention
form a picture in your mind
get discouraged about
get the most from (something)
have a positive attitude
jog your memory
jot down (something)
kinesthetic (type of learner)
make associations
paraphrase
prepare (yourself) mentally
retain information
take a break
visual (type of learner)
warm up

Chapter 2

agree with
apply
contribute to
emphasize
essay test
exchange
familiar with
find out
focus on
footnotes
form a group
good luck charm
graphs
hints
ignore
incomplete
landmarks
make a good impression
mark
material
multiple choice test
nightmare

open-book test
penalized
prepare for
pretend
remind
require
short-answer test
statement
study group
watch out for
well rested

Chapter 3

an/one example is
are connected to
bank
be accompanied by
beasts
bind
brought about
channel
commodities
consulted with
cross-cultural exchange
empire
extensive
fiber
flows out
for example
for instance
manes
marveled at
precious stones
primitive
ran from ... to
resembles
reveal
silk routes
spread across
state
such as
takes on
taking (them) to be
technological benefit
travel along (road/route/river/sea)
travel by (means of transportation)
travel for (time)

travel from (place) to (specific
place)/through (region)
X is an example of

Chapter 4

adventurers
aerodynamics forces
aviation
bat
break the sound barrier
cockpit
concealed
covered a distance of (a distance)
dimensions
drag
excerpted
fight against
fixed
flew across (a place)
flew over (a place)
fly over (a speed)
furnish
fuselage
gliders
infinite
lift
linear
locomotion
on board
personal
propel
provides
replica
resume
sailed forward
thrust
trial
wrecked

Chapter 5

accept
accountant
alternate
appropriately
aspects
assigns

commission
creative thinking
criticize
decision-making
evaluating alternatives
extrovert
introvert
knowing how to learn
leader
logic
messes up
participate in
patiently
percentages
problem-solving
rearrange
refuse
revise
self-esteem
self-image
swings
thinking skills
trust

Chapter 6

analyze
associations
(be) familiar with
brand loyalty
branding
choose to do business
conformity
consumers
corporations
decide to buy
effectively
entering a market
evaluate
have in common
hope to sell
manufacturer
market
marketers
marketing
model
need to fit
planned to market
poked fun at
retailer
slogan

values
wants to sell

Chapter 7

are next to
asteroid
astrogeologists
astronomy
axis
conflicts
denser
detected
drastically
evidence
extermination
fly slowly over
hematite
impact
infer
inspired
invaders
is/are less... than
is/are more...than
is/are (much) ... -er than
just like
make observations about
moved upward from
orbiting
panic
parallel
reflects
slant
subsurface
the same as
themes
threatening
travels along
warrior
which contain

Chapter 8

atmospheric conditions
based on
bounce
caught in
chances are
climate
consistent
data

estimating
exhilarating
factor
flagpole
grains
humidity
inadvertently
interpolation
keep track of
outlets
persistence
recognizable
redevelop
require forecasters to
shelters
struck by
survive
sweep you off your feet
taken into consideration
takes about
trend
typically
weather fronts

Chapter 9

at + age
blessed
bucks
butler
by + period of time or specific time
caterer
combo
derived from
ensemble
entrepreneur
festivals
from (time) to (time)
heritages
illiterate
improvisation
in + period of time
instrumentalist
merges
mold
on + specific date
oppressed
pampered
restrict
rural
solo

Skills Index

Academic Word List

To help you increase your vocabulary we have included Sublist One of the most common words on the Academic Word List, a list compiled by Averil Coxhead. To view the entire list, go to the School of Linguistics and Applied Language Studies website (www.vuw.ac.nz/lals/research/awl/).

Each word in italics is the most frequently occurring member of the word family in the Academic Corpus. For example, *analysis* is the most common form of the word family analyse.

analyse
  analysed
  analyser
  analysers
  analyses
  analysing
  analysis
  analyst
  analysts
  analytic
  analytical
  analytically
  analyze
  analyzed
  analyzes
  analyzing
approach
  approachable
  approached
  approaches
  approaching
  unapproachable
area
  areas
assess
  assessable
  assessed
  assesses
  assessing
  assessment
  assessments
  reassess
  reassessed
  reassessing
  reassessment
  unassessed

assume
  assumed
  assumes
  assuming
  assumption
  assumptions
authority
  authoritative
  authorities
available
  availability
  unavailable
benefit
  beneficial
  beneficiary
  beneficiaries
  benefited
  benefiting
  benefits
concept
  conception
  concepts
  conceptual
  conceptualisation
  conceptualise
  conceptualised
  conceptualises
  conceptualising
  conceptually
consist
  consisted
  consistency
  consistent
  consistently
  consisting
  consists

  inconsistencies
  inconsistency
  inconsistent
constitute
  constituencies
  constituency
  constituent
  constituents
  constituted
  constitutes
  constituting
  constitution
  constitutions
  constitutional
  constitutionally
  constitutive
  unconstitutional
context
  contexts
  contextual
  contextualise
  contextualised
  contextualising
  uncontextualised
  contextualize
  contextualized
  contextualizing
  uncontextualized
contract
  contracted
  contracting
  contractor
  contractors
  contracts
create
  created

creates
creating
creation
creations
creative
creatively
creativity
creator
creators
recreate
recreated
recreates
recreating
data
define
  definable
  defined
  defines
  defining
  definition
  definitions
  redefine
  redefined
  redefines
  redefining
  undefined
derive
  derivation
  derivations
  derivative
  derivatives
  derived
  derives
  deriving
distribute
  distributed
  distributing
  distribution
  distributional
  distributions
  distributive
  distributor
  distributors

redistribute
redistributed
redistributes
redistributing
redistribution
economy
  economic
  economical
  economically
  economics
  economies
  economist
  economists
  uneconomical
environment
  environmental
  environmentalist
  environmentalists
  environmentally
  environments
establish
  disestablish
  disestablished
  disestablishes
  disestablishing
  disestablishment
  established
  establishes
  establishing
  establishment
  establishments
estimate
  estimated
  estimates
  estimating
  estimation
  estimations
  over-estimate
  overestimate
  overestimated
  overestimates
  overestimating
  underestimate

underestimated
underestimates
underestimating
evident
  evidenced
  evidence
  evidential
  evidently
export
  exported
  exporter
  exporters
  exporting
  exports
factor
  factored
  factoring
  factors
finance
  financed
  finances
  financial
  financially
  financier
  financiers
  financing
formula
  formulae
  formulas
  formulate
  formulated
  formulating
  formulation
  formulations
  reformulate
  reformulated
  reformulating
  reformulation
  reformulations
function
  functional
  functionally
  functioned

functioning
functions
identify
  identifiable
  identification
  identified
  identifies
  identifying
  identities
  identity
  unidentifiable
income
  incomes
indicate
  indicated
  indicates
  indicating
  indication
  indications
  indicative
  indicator
  indicators
individual
  individualised
  individuality
  individualism
  individualist
  individualists
  individualistic
  individually
  individuals
interpret
  interpretation
  interpretations
  interpretative
  interpreted
  interpreting
  interpretive
  interprets
  misinterpret
  misinterpretation
  misinterpretations
  misinterpreted

misinterpreting
misinterprets
reinterpret
reinterpreted
reinterprets
reinterpreting
reinterpretation
reinterpretations
involve
  involved
  involvement
  involves
  involving
  uninvolved
issue
  issued
  issues
  issuing
labour
  labor
  labored
  labors
  laboured
  labouring
  labours
legal
  illegal
  illegality
  illegally
  legality
  legally
legislate
  legislated
  legislates
  legislating
  legislation
  legislative
  legislator
  legislators
  legislature
major
  majorities
  majority

method
  methodical
  methodological
  methodologies
  methodology
  methods
occur
  occurred
  occurrence
  occurrences
  occurring
  occurs
  reoccur
  reoccurred
  reoccurring
  reoccurs
percent
  percentage
  percentages
period
  periodic
  periodical
  periodically
  periodicals
  periods
policy
  policies
principle
  principled
  principles
  unprincipled
proceed
  procedural
  procedure
  procedures
  proceeded
  proceeding
  proceedings
  proceeds
process
  processed
  processes
  processing

require
  required
  requirement
  requirements
  requires
  requiring
research
  researched
  researcher
  researchers
  researches
  researching
respond
  responded
  respondent
  respondents
  responding
  responds
  response
  responses
  responsive
  responsiveness
  unresponsive
role
  roles
section
  sectioned
  sectioning
  sections

sector
  sectors
significant
  insignificant
  insignificantly
  significance
  significantly
  signified
  signifies
  signify
  signifying
similar
  dissimilar
  similarities
  similarity
  similarly
source
  sourced
  sources
  sourcing
specific
  specifically
  specification
  specifications
  specificity
  specifics
structure
  restructure
  restructured

restructures
restructuring
structural
structurally
structured
structures
structuring
unstructured
theory
  theoretical
  theoretically
  theories
  theorist
  theorists
vary
  invariable
  invariably
  variability
  variable
  variables
  variably
  variance
  variant
  variants
  variation
  variations
  varied
  varies
  varying

Frequency Word List

Below are the most common words in English, compiled by Edward Bernard Fry, Jacqueline E. Kress and Dona Lee Fountoukidis.

These most commonly used words are ranked by frequency. The first 25 make up about one-third of all printed material in English. The first 100 make up about one-half of all written material, and the first 300 make up about 65 percent of all written material in English.

1. the	36. we	71. two
2. of	37. when	72. more
3. and	38. your	73. write
4. a	39. can	74. go
5. to	40. said	75. see
6. in	41. there	76. number
7. is	42. use	77. no
8. you	43. an	78. way
9. that	44. each	79. could
10. it	45. which	80. people
11. he	46. she	81. my
12. was	47. do	82. than
13. for	48. how	83. first
14. on	49. their	84. water
15. are	50. if	85. been
16. as	51. will	86. call
17. with	52. up	87. who
18. his	53. other	88. oil
19. they	54. about	89. its
20. I	55. out	90. now
21. at	56. many	91. find
22. be	57. then	92. long
23. this	58. them	93. down
24. have	59. these	94. day
25. from	60. so	95. did
26. or	61. some	96. get
27. one	62. her	97. come
28. had	63. would	98. made
29. by	64. make	99. may
30. word	65. like	100. part
31. but	66. him	101. over
32. not	67. into	102. new
33. what	68. time	103. sound
34. all	69. has	104. take
35. were	70. look	105. only

106. little	150. small	194. found
107. work	151. set	195. study
108. know	152. put	196. still
109. place	153. end	197. learn
110. year	154. does	198. should
111. live	155. another	199. America
112. me	156. well	200. world
113. back	157. large	201. high
114. give	158. must	202. every
115. most	159. big	203. near
116. very	160. even	204. add
117. after	161. such	205. food
118. thing	162. because	206. between
119. our	163. turn	207. own
120. just	164. here	208. below
121. name	165. why	209. country
122. good	166. ask	210. plant
123. sentence	167. went	211. last
124. man	168. men	212. school
125. think	169. read	213. father
126. say	170. need	214. keep
127. great	171. land	215. tree
128. where	172. different	216. never
129. help	173. home	217. start
130. through	174. us	218. city
131. much	175. move	219. earth
132. before	176. try	220. eye
133. line	177. kind	221. light
134. right	178. hand	222. thought
135. too	179. picture	223. head
136. mean	180. again	224. under
137. old	181. change	225. story
138. any	182. off	226. saw
139. same	183. play	227. left
140. tell	184. spell	228. don't
141. boy	185. air	229. few
142. follow	186. away	230. while
143. came	187. animal	231. along
144. want	188. house	232. might
145. show	189. point	233. close
146. also	190. page	234. something
147. around	191. letter	235. seem
148. form	192. mother	236. next
149. three	193. answer	237. hard

238. open	282. far	326. order
239. example	283. Indian	327. red
240. begin	284. really	328. door
241. life	285. almost	329. sure
242. always	286. let	330. become
243. those	287. above	331. top
244. both	288. girl	332. ship
245. paper	289. sometimes	333. across
246. together	290. mountain	334. today
247. got	291. cut	335. during
248. group	292. young	336. short
249. often	293. talk	337. better
250. run	294. soon	338. best
251. important	295. list	339. however
252. until	296. song	340. low
253. children	297. being	341. hours
254. side	298. leave	342. black
255. feet	299. family	343. products
256. car	300. it's	344. happened
257. mile	301. body	345. whole
258. night	302. music	346. measure
259. walk	303. color	347. remember
260. white	304. stand	348. early
261. sea	305. sun	349. waves
262. began	306. questions	350. reached
263. grow	307. fish	351. listen
264. took	308. area	352. wind
265. river	309. mark	353. rock
266. four	310. dog	354. space
267. carry	311. horse	355. covered
268. state	312. birds	356. fast
269. once	313. problem	357. several
270. book	314. complete	358. hold
271. hear	315. room	359. himself
272. stop	316. knew	360. toward
273. without	317. since	361. five
274. second	318. ever	362. step
275. later	319. piece	363. morning
276. miss	320. told	364. passed
277. idea	321. usually	365. vowel
278. enough	322. didn't	366. true
279. eat	323. friends	367. hundred
280. face	324. easy	368. against
281. watch	325. heard	369. pattern

370. numeral
371. table
372. north
373. slowly
374. money
375. map
376. farm
377. pulled
378. draw
379. voice
380. seen
381. cold
382. cried
383. plan
384. notice
385. south
386. sing
387. war
388. ground
389. fall
390. king
391. town
392. I'll
393. unit
394. figure
395. certain
396. field
397. travel
398. wood
399. fire
400. upon
401. done
402. English
403. road
404. halt
405. ten
406. fly
407. gave
408. box
409. finally
410. wait
411. correct
412. oh
413. quickly

414. person
415. became
416. shown
417. minutes
418. strong
419. verb
420. stars
421. front
422. feel
423. fact
424. inches
425. street
426. decided
427. contain
428. course
429. surface
430. produce
431. building
432. ocean
433. class
434. note
435. nothing
436. rest
437. carefully
438. scientists
439. inside
440. wheels
441. stay
442. green
443. known
444. island
445. week
446. less
447. machine
448. base
449. ago
450. stood
451. plane
452. system
453. behind
454. ran
455. round
456. boat
457. game

458. force
459. brought
460. understand
461. warm
462. common
463. bring
464. explain
465. dry
466. though
467. language
468. shape
469. deep
470. thousands
471. yes
472. clear
473. equation
474. yet
475. government
476. filled
477. heat
478. full
479. hot
480. check
481. object
482. am
483. rule
484. among
485. noun
486. power
487. cannot
488. able
489. six
490. size
491. dark
492. ball
493. material
494. special
495. heavy
496. fine
497. pair
498. circle
499. include
500. built

Text Credits

pp. 14, 30, and 35 From Peak Performance Success in College and Beyond 4e by Sharon K. Ferrett, 2000. Reprinted by permission of the McGraw-Hill Companies. p. 54 From "IBN Battuta: Long Distance Traveler" from *Travels in Asia and Africa, 1325–1354* translated by H.A.R. Gibb. Reprinted by permission of Thomson Publishing Services, on behalf of Taylor and Francis Books. p. 59 Excerpt adapted "Cross-Cultural Exchange: 1000–1500" *from Traditions and Encounters: A Global Perspective on the Past* 2e by Jerry H. Bentley, 2003. Reprinted by permission of the McGraw-Hill Companies. p. 76 Adapted from "On Flight by Orville and Wilbur Wright", *San Francisco Chronicle*, December 14, 2003. © San Francisco Chronicle. Reprinted by permission. p. 151 Excerpt adapted "The Geology of Mars" from *Explorations: An Introduction to Astronomy*, updated 3e by Thomas Arny, 2002. Reprinted by permission of the McGraw-Hill Companies p. 173 Excerpt "How Weather Prediction Works" from *Meteorology*, 2e by Eric William Danielson, 2003. Reprinted by permission of the McGraw-Hill Companies. p. 216 From The Freer Gallery of Art and Arthur M. Sackler Gallery website - www.asia.si.edu. Reprinted by permission. p. 220 Excerpts "Crossing Cultures: Japonisme and Western Art" from *Gilbert's Living with Art,* 6e by Mark Getlein, 2001, pp. 101, 249, 469, & 496. Reprinted by permission of the McGraw-Hill Companies. p. 244 From Averl Coxhead, the School of Linguistics and Applied Language Studies at Victoria University of Wellington, New Zealand. Reprinted by permission of Averil Coxhead. p. 248 From *The Reading Teacher's Book of Lists* by Edward Bernard Fry, Jacqueline E. Kress and Dona Lee Fountoukidis, 2000.

Photo Credits

From the Getty Images Royalty-Free Collection: p. 4, left; p. 4, right; p. 7; p. 8, left; p. 8, right; p. 16; p. 26, left; p. 26, right; p. 28; p. 36, bottom; p. 44; p. 48; p. 54, bottom; p. 58; p. 61, top; p. 72, left; p. 90, top; p. 90, center left; p. 90, center right; p. 90, bottom left; p. 90, bottom right; p. 94; p. 96, left; p. 96, right; p. 99, center; p. 99, right; p. 106; p. 107; p. 118, left; p. 118, right; p. 122; p. 140; p. 142, left; p. 143; p. 151, top; p. 164, left; p. 164, right; p. 168, top; p. 210, right; p. 212, photo 3; p. 212, photo 4;

From the CORBIS Royalty-Free Collection: p. 2; p. 6; p. 35; p. 36, top; p. 54, top; p. 61, bottom right; p. 68; p. 76, bottom; p. 79; p. 81; p. 86; p. 99, left; p. 165; p. 168, bottom; p. 169; p. 173, Figure 1; p. 173, Figure 2; p. 174; p. 182; p. 212, photo 1; p. 212, photo 2;

Other Images: cover, top left: Axel Hoedt/Getty Images; cover, top right: Anne Ackermann/Getty Images; cover, bottom left: Pictor/Imagestate; cover, bottom right: Ghislain & Marie David de Lossy/Getty Images; p. 59: Hulton-Deutsch Collection/CORBIS; p. 61, bottom left: Chris Hellier/CORBIS; p. 72, right: Library of Congress; p. 74: Library of Congress; p. 82, top: Underwood & Underwood/CORBIS; p. 82, bottom: Bettmann/CORBIS; p. 115: Syracuse Newspapers/The Image Works; *p.* 127, left: Annebicque Bernard/CORBIS SYGMA; p. 127, middle: James Leynse/CORBIS; p. 127, right: Getty Images; p. 136: McGraw-Hill Companies, Inc./Gary He, photographer; p. 142, right: Warner Bros./The Kobal Collection; p. 146: 20th Century Fox/The Kobal Collection; p. 151, middle: NASA; p. 151, bottom: NASA/USGS; p. 152, Figure 7.4: NASA/JPL/MSSS; p. 152, Figure 7.5: NASA; p. 152, Figure 7.6: NASA/JPL; p. 152, Figure 7.7: NASA/JPL/Malin Space Science Systems; p. 153, top: NASA/JPL/Malin Space Science Systems; p. 173, Figure 3: National Centers for Environmental Prediction; p. 186: Mel Curtis/Getty Images; p. 188, left: Gary Hershorn/Reuters/CORBIS ; p. 188, right: Bettmann/CORBIS; p. 192: Bettmann/CORBIS; p. 197: Getty Images; p. 198: Gary Hershorn/Reuters/CORBIS ; p. 199: AFP/Getty Images; p. 206: Getty Images; p. 210, left: Christie's Images/CORBIS; p. 213: David Grossman/Photo Researchers, Inc.; p. 219: Erich Lessing/Art Resource, NY; p. 220, left: Tate Gallery, London/Art Resource, NY; p. 220, right: Christie's Images/CORBIS; p. 221: Christie's Images/CORBIS; p. 222, left: Philadelphia Museum of Art/CORBIS; p. 222, right: Scala/Art Resource, NY; p. 226: Snark/Art Resource, NY; p. 230: Christie's Images/CORBIS.

We apologize for any apparent infringement of copyright and if notified, the publisher will be pleased to rectify any errors or omissions at the earliest opportunity.